THE MESSAGE OF
THE MASS MELODIES

THE MESSAGE

OF THE

MASS MELODIES

by

John C. Murrett, M.M.

OS JUSTI
PRESS

Nihil Obstat
John Eidenschink, O.S.B., J.C.D.
Censor Deputatus

Imprimatur
✠ Peter W. Bartholome, D.D.
Bishop of St. Cloud
January 23, 1960

The Message of the Mass Melodies
was originally published in 1960
by The Liturgical Press, Collegeville,
with a copyright by the Catholic Foreign Mission Society of America
(The Maryknoll Fathers), Maryknoll, New York.
The present book is an exact reproduction of that edition,
which is in the public domain.

Os Justi Press
P.O. Box 21814
Lincoln, NE 68542
www.osjustipress.com

Send inquiries to
info@osjustipress.com

ISBN 978-1-965303-56-6 (paperback)
ISBN 978-1-965303-57-3 (hardcover)

Cover design: Julian Kwasniewski

TO SAINT PIUS TENTH
Roman Pontiff
filled with a burning desire to see
the true Christian spirit flourish
in the liturgy of the Church
this book is humbly dedicated.

ACKNOWLEDGMENTS

Most of the excerpts from the psalms are taken from a book now out of print, *The Psalms*, by Abbot Smith, O.S.B. Other Biblical texts are adaptations from Monsignor Knox's Bible, and still a few others are translations by Father Mark Kent, M.M. The quotations from Dom Johner's *Chants of the Vatican Gradual* are given with the permission of the St. John's Abbey Press, Collegeville, Minnesota.

Some may feel that contained within these pages are expressions, phrases, or passages taken from Pius Parsch's works, from Father Emeric Lawrence's *The Week with Christ*, or from other sources. That may be true. If it is, I apologize, but must say that I did not wilfully plagiarize these sources: I have used all of them so often and have become so familiar with them over the years that I may have inadvertently expressed my own thoughts in their words. To all of them I am much indebted for ideas and inspirations.

Note: Choir directors will find it helpful to use the *Liber Usualis* or *Graduales* together with these comments.

INTRODUCTION

Liturgists are always reminding us that Church music is but the handmaid of the liturgy, and that is as it should be. Yet it has always seemed to me that the musical compositions created originally for the rendition of various chants have gone one step further: they have been composed in such a way that, in most of the approved music, the meaning of the words has been enhanced and made clearer by the music. Two of the most beautiful examples of this—two that started me on a quest I began more than thirty years ago—are the Gregorian *Ave Maria* and the *Salve Regina* (simplex).

What struck me first of all was how like "Hello" or any other familiar term of greeting was the music of *Ave*; and I went on to see the *Maria* winding up into heaven, where our Lady is so far above us. Then, one cannot but feel the fullness of the *gratia* in *gratia plena*, and the *dicta tu*—not in heaven, but down on earth among *mulieribus*. Wonder lies beneath the words and music that follow—only to rise to great, almost incomprehensible awe in *Jesus*. *Sancta Maria* is a cry from the hearts of fearful children, but it is softened in *Mater Dei*. Then hear the pleading in *ora pro nobis*, when we ask our Lady to look down and see how low is our estate (*peccatoribus*). The *nunc* is bright as we realize that we still have time to work out our salvation "now while it is day"; but quickly that changes to remind us of the desperate need we have of her intercession *in hora mortis nostrae*, when we may not be able to pray for ourselves. The whispered "So be it" of the *Amen* is very humble and trusting.

The same is equally true of the *Salve Regina*. See how the *Regina* takes us up to heaven, where Mary is Queen of the world; the buoyancy in *vita*, and the sweetness of *dulcedo*, and the humble realization of *spes nostrae*. Our cry goes up (*ad te clamamus*), we who are *filii Hevae* down on earth, not overjoyed, but *gementes et flentes* in the depths of *hoc lacrymarum valle*. *Ergo*, we go up to our *advocata*, and we can see her tenderly turning her eyes in *illos tuos* and *oculos* away down to us (*ad nos converte*). But that glance of mercy gives us courage to rise again in *Et Jesum*: hold Him up to look down on us (*ostende*). What music could express more clearly the clemency, the holiness, the dignity of our *Virgo Maria?*

I present these two examples first of all because they were the two compositions that introduced me to what seemed a hidden beauty; besides, they are familiar to most choirs who sing Gregorian music. However, what is found here is true of most of the music contained in the *Liber Usualis* or other *Graduales.*

In these pages I have tried only to point out how beautifully the liturgy of Sundays and holydays is enchanced by the music of the Introit, Gradual, Offertory, and Communion. Father A. M. Romb, O.F.M. Conv., in his *Understanding Chant*,[1] states: "It goes without saying that the subject matter or form of chant is the material of faith itself.... Chant was written to accommodate the text.... The cadences of chant even coincide with the phrasing and logic of the text. More than any other music with lyrics can chant be termed 'heightened speech.' The music is truly subservient to the words it accompanies." Again, in the same work we read: "Emotion is expressed *through music*...yet the emotion should not arise *from the music*...but should overflow from the mind's understanding and the will's conviction about the meaning of the text."

If those in charge of weekly choir and chant rehearsals will take but a few minutes to help the singers consider these ideas, they will find that a better appreciation of the liturgy will result, and that those persons who are so privileged to lift up their voices to God will be led to a greater love of Him.

[1] The Liturgical Press, Collegeville, Minn.

CONTENTS

TEMPORAL CYCLE

FIRST SUNDAY OF ADVENT

The Gospel sounds the keynote not only of this Sunday but of all Advent. "Look up, and lift up your heads," our Lord bids us, "because your redemption is at hand." The consolation of that message fills all our Advent days with great hope. God is coming to redeem us, to free our souls from all that would deprive them of His grace. So we exclaim in the

INTROIT – Psalm 24:1-4.

"To You, O Lord, I lift up my soul. I beg You to give me this grace, that I may be able to lift my soul to You. You alone, Lord, can save me from the shame of forgetting You. If I attempt this by my own power, I shall surely fail, and my enemies, the evil spirits, will triumph over me; but all who trust in You shall be saved from confusion. Show me Your ways, O Lord, by letting me understand Your precepts; enable me to walk always according to Your will."

Advent reminds us that by His incarnation Christ will become *Deus meus*. It sounds so exalted! Lift up your heads—your redemption is at hand! Redemption will come when the Son of Man comes, and all the earth will see that those who trust in Him are never confounded. All our yearnings will be granted; all the desires of the human heart (*exspectant*) will find their complete satisfaction in God. My soul is all that matters. See *animam meam*—it is like a reverent look at God; and *meam* is indicative of childlike submission. The *confido* is so full of confidence that the *non* following it is triumphant; so with *neque*, and so forth. The prayer almost becomes a command: "Lord, because of my confidence in You, You cannot do otherwise than help me against my enemies." Confident expectation is thus brought to the fore, with the conviction that the preceding petitions will be granted. How beautifully our song becomes a prayer, lifting up our hearts (*levavi*) to God!

The Gradual, Alleluia, and Offertory of today's Mass "pound" those same thoughts home to us by repetition. Notice especially the feelings expressed by the music for these words:

1

universi—high, and low, and wide; *exspectant*—impatient. See the reverence in the first five notes of *Domine* (there are two instances), and then the rising of the soul as we begin to understand the privilege of even being able to call upon His Name. The *mihi* goes to great heights, but the thought of God teaching me (*edoce*) becomes more seriously respectful: *me*—a person who has fallen often from grace. No wonder that the salvation given to us (*salutare...da nobis*) raises our hopes.

OFFERTORY – Psalm 24:1-3.

"O Lord, to You have I lifted...." Even more clearly than in the Introit, the melody here lifts itself from the depths, even though it keeps within the four lines; and as we glance at it, immediately there is something restful about its appearance. It looks easy! The melody here is more subdued than at the Introit. Perhaps the Secret that follows, perhaps the beautiful Act at the altar exerts its influence upon this Offertory song. "All who expect You" to come down to them (note the end of *exspectant*) are quiet and serene in their confidence. Then, when we have tasted of the harvest of the Sacrifice, we are well able to sing of goodness and fruit in the

COMMUNION – Psalm 84:13.

"It is for You, O Lord, to give me Your own goodness, that my heart may bear fruit pleasing to You." Our Lord has blessed us by coming into our souls, and our joy is reflected in the melody of these words. Dom Johner notes in this instance: "A joyous animation runs through the melody with these words. What copious blessings has the Lord poured upon this earth, and what a plenitude of grace has He again placed in our souls in Holy Communion as seed for eternity! Wherever this seed falls upon rich soil, in souls who recognize that the one thing necessary is to do the will of God, there it bears rich fruit."[1]

See how the music resembles God's grace raining down upon our souls, the grace which God so generously gives to those who are in accord with Him. Some English missals translate *benignitatem* as "goodness," but it is much more than that: a benign person spreads himself; he is gentle, kind, and very generous.

[1] *Chants of the Vatican Gradual*, p. 20.

Even the notes indicate that feeling. So may we conclude: If during each day's advent we look with confidence to Him who is our expectation, He will gladly protect us against our enemies; and He will drop down His fruit, *dabit fructum suum*, into our souls, that we may be strengthened thereby to rise to a new life with Him.

SECOND SUNDAY OF ADVENT

This is the Sunday of heralds and messengers. The Gospel tells of St. John the Baptist sending two of his disciples to ask Jesus, "Are You He who is to come?" And Jesus speaks of John as His messenger who would "prepare the way." Advent points out the value of being heralds and messengers to prepare Christ's way in the hearts of men.

We most truly prepare the way by first being sure that the way to our own hearts is open to receive our Lord, that there is no stubble amidst the straw in the mangers of our hearts. Hence, we give our attention to what is proclaimed in the

INTROIT – Isaias 30:30.

"O you people of Sion, listen: Behold, the Lord is rising from the earth, from the fleshly body of one of His creatures— He, the Lord, the highest is coming! He is coming! He is coming not only to redeem you, but He shall make the glory of His voice heard in the joy of your heart. Be aware of this, all of you, and give glory to the Father, and to the Son, and to the Holy Spirit."

At rehearsal, let the organist sound two or three times the music for *Populus Sion*. Note how like a trumpet call it is, calling the people to attention. Then note the awe in the music of *veniet*; it is truly beyond our comprehension that for our sake He comes. And the purpose of His coming? To save all nations of the earth! The descending notes show His incomparable condescension; and again the music seems hushed with awe by such a truth.

Once more the opening trumpet call is heard, to bid us remember that we are listening to a great message. The *et auditum* seems to say: "Hear ye, He is coming not only to redeem you, but also to bring joy to your heart by the sound of His voice!"

Faciet Dominus—God in heaven shall do this; see how the notes of the music here keep that thought clearly before us. It does not seem difficult to imagine the heaven-high tones of His glorious voice. Let one chanter sing *gloriam vocis suae* alone, softly; then two or three repeat it; then all. What keeps our joyful hearts from overflowing? What must the sound of His voice be in heaven? Our hearts are high; our joy is snatched from heaven for a brief moment, before the *vestri* brings us down to earth again.

GRADUAL – Psalm 49:2-3,5.[1]

"From His own land God shall come, showing us the loveliness of His beauty. You, His saints, who hold His law of love greater than any sacrifice you can make, come and gather together, and with songs of praise to Him who is (Alleluia), rejoice at what is promised: You shall one day enter into the house of the Lord." The Introit promised that when the Lord comes, He will bring joy to our hearts; and the Epistle ended with the prayer of that great lover, St. Paul: "Now may the God of hope fill you with every joy"; and these same ideas are contained and embellished in the Gradual.

Note how *ex Sion* seems to rise from the people of Israel, and yet remains a short while with them. The loveliness of His beauty finds expression in the music; and then see how uplifting is that on the word *Deus*—a very short phrase to be separated, as if it were bidding us to think of God alone. In *manifeste veniet* we can see Him coming, born of one of us, coming down to the very lowest of His earth. *Congregate* spreads out to gather all the ends of the earth together; and although the beauty of *illi sanctos* shows us how privileged we are, the *ejus* reminds us of the valley in which we dwell as we work out our salvation, preparing for His coming.

Notice that the melody of *species* is repeated in the ending of *testamentum ejus*: His loveliness reflected in the gospel of love. Another repetition, *super sacrificia*, is very much like *illi sanctos*: the sacrifice made by His saints in order to progress in love shall not go unrewarded even in this life, where His joy will fill their hearts. Hear the joy of *laetatus*, the sound of His voice in *dicta*,

[1] Father Mark Kent's translation.

the humility in *mihi*. And see all His saints rising to His house (*domum*) with the calm peacefulness of *Domini*, contentment in His presence. *Ibimus* continues the thought of our rising in *domum*, until we finally come to rest.

OFFERTORY — Psalm 84:7-8.

"Give to me, my God, a full, vigorous, spiritual life; then shall my heart rejoice with true joy in You. Show me Your mercy, my own good God, for without Your help I cannot be safe." Again a trumpet call is sounded, assuring us that God will turn His face towards His people, and that when He comes, He will bring the kind of life that will fill us with joy—life in Him and with Him.

He will be merciful and will save us when our lack of love makes us forget the great boon that is ours. See how many evidences of these thoughts are to be found in the various groups of notes. Outstanding is *misericordiam tuam*: we need His mercy when we let our souls cling to the earth. There is a brief surge of hope on the syllable *cor*, as though we are reminded that we can count on His mercy, the mercy of His sacred Heart; but then we come right down to earth again, realizing our dependence upon Him.

COMMUNION — Baruch 5:5; 4:36.

"Arise, O Jerusalem, and stand enrapt as you see the joy that comes to you from your God." There is another clarion call for Israel to rouse itself in *surge*. How easy it is to see the joy coming down from heaven on *quae veniet tibi*. In the holy Sacrifice Christ has just come down from heaven and into our hearts, and the music is subdued. All the glorious strains of which we have been singing are now coursing through our souls, for we have given ear, and God has turned and come down with His salvation; we have been given the promise of so great an advent that is one day to be ours. And all of this through the loving mercy *a Deo tuo*.

THIRD SUNDAY OF ADVENT

Last Sunday we were bidden to surfeit our souls in joy of spirit because of our Lord's coming. The joy to which we are called today is one that is emphasized with outward expression: flowers, rose-colored vestments, and the sound of the organ contribute their share, and we are invited to lift our voices—not too high, lest that would smack of empty joy—but with a gladness that "let's courtesy be known."

INTROIT – Philippians 4:4-6.

"Rejoice in the Lord always; again I say, rejoice. Let your moderation be known to all men. The Lord is near. Have no anxiety, but in every prayer let your petitions be made known to God." Notice how moderately calm is the music of *Gaudete*, until it begins to rise to God *in Domino semper*. Joy in God is a very high and noble thing; and although "again I say rejoice," note the sobriety of *iterum dico gaudete*. "Once again I wish you joy" is the expression of soul that we give to one another as we sing to the Lord.

For *modestia* Monsignor Knox writes: "Give proof of your courtesy"; his translation helps us to understand better each phrase of the music. *Modestia vestra* shows a graceful rising that continues on an even level for *omnibus hominibus*—all men, regardless of race, color, country, or creed. What a happy world it would be if all who read or sing or say those words today were to observe that advice—"Give proof of your courtesy"—which bids us to give to others some of the love that God has given to us.

See our *oratione* rising to God, but our *petitiones* concern ourselves and others who are on earth with us. *Apud* lifts us, and yet it brings us to solemnity at the sacred word *Deum*. The joy in this Introit is much more restrained than was last Sunday's. We are getting nearer to the birth of the divine Babe. The liturgy today almost tells us to approach Him quietly, serenely, so as not to disturb Him.

GRADUAL – Psalm 79:2-3.

Study this paraphrase: "O God, who reigns so high above the Cherubim, look at us down here on earth, who can scarcely

6

lift our eyes or our voices, but in a low whisper beg of You to please use Your great power and come down to us, and be one of us. I am sure, O Lord, that You will hear our prayer and come; because I recall that You did not forsake Israel when Your people needed You, but like the Good Shepherd that You are, You led them as sheep to safety. Oh, how our souls are lifted to You as we recall Your great mercies! Our faith gives us so much confidence that we must sing *Alleluia*!"

Looking over the musical notes and remembering these words, we find it very easy to see how truly the music lends force to the ideas. See *Domine* enthroned on high, so far *super* the Cherubim, who, nevertheless, are much higher than we are. On the syllable *-bim* one can almost see the angels flying around the foundation of God's throne! Today's composers would probably be inclined to make the music of *potentiam tuam* more powerful, but St. Gregory put courtesy before everything else. There is compliment (adoration and faith) enough in the words, a pompous arrangment would have made it something akin to servile flattery.

In *qui regis Israel* we see the soul rising gradually to the God of Israel and then wandering down again with Joseph, the young shepherd in the valley below. We humbly express our faith, and then the soul rises as an irrepressible joy fills our *Alleluia*. On the first Sunday of Advent we pleaded with God to "stir up" His power and come to us. Today this same thought is repeated, as if we would have our Lord understand that we truly mean what we are saying. Confidence in having our prayer granted is expressed in the joyfulness of the melody: first in the *Alleluia*, and then again in *Domine*, and finally in *facias nos*.

OFFERTORY – Psalm 84:2,3.

"How good You have been to me, O my God! You have blessed me and freed me from being captivated by the things of the world. Through the passion of Your Son, in Your mercy, You have washed away our sins in the sacrament of penance." In the music it is not difficult to picture the blessings of heaven falling to the earth, the rising to God on *Domine*, and the descent on *terram*. But then we cannot but note how calmly the melody goes along with moderation and a sense of security.

While the offering is being made at the altar, we know that there is nothing to fear, if we but liberate our wills to the will of God. We can even refer to our *iniquitatem* in tones that are not depressed, because confidence, faith, and love have assured us of God's redeeming sacrifice for our sake. Then, doubly assured by having received the Food of angels, our seeming boldness wants to cry out in the

COMMUNION – Isaias 35:4.

"O you fainthearted people, take courage! Do not be afraid; our God *will* come and save us." This is a beautiful chant with which to close the holy Sacrifice today. It is one that we want to shout from the housetops. See *ecce*, which seems to urge us to "look up," and the strength of *veniet*, assuring us that He *will* come down from heaven and *salvabit nos*. In every difficulty, in every disturbing moment, what a consolation it can be for us to recall this Sunday's liturgy! We are free, with a freedom bought for us by God coming down from heaven. Therefore, let our souls always rise in a hearty *Gaudete*!

FOURTH SUNDAY OF ADVENT

INTROIT – Isaias 45:8.

"O ye heavens, bedew the earth from above, and let the clouds rain down the just one, the Savior. May He, springing forth from the closed womb of the earth, bring true, right order to His firmament." *Rorate* is often translated "drop down dew"; but from the music of St. Gregory in this instance, "bedew" seems more fitting. A lesson in agronomy: Dew does not actually drop down of its own accord, but the warm earth at night draws moisture out of the atmosphere to refresh and purify plants and flowers, and help them to bud forth. The rain clouds, too, send refreshing showers that sink down to the roots.

In *Rorate* see the earth reaching up to draw down the Dew of eternal life; see the height of the heavens above in *caeli desuper*, and the lower clouds (*nubes*). Then follow the rain as it starts down in *pluant* to bring us the Just One. There is great tenderness in that *justum*. Then note the opening (*aperiatur*) of the lowly *terra*. The translation of *et germinet* is often given as "and bud forth"; but actually "germinate" would be better, because germination means that a seed, after being buried in the earth and watered by dew and rain, begins to push a tiny green blade above the earth—and then the bud, and then the flower. It is easier to understand the music on *salvatorem* from that point of view. Perhaps St. Gregory wanted to show, too, that our Lord, coming as Savior, was taking His beginning from a creature of the earth. He comes from the earth, to save His earthly creatures, the work of His hands.

GRADUAL — Psalm 144:18,21.

"You are very near to us, Lord, when we call upon You, speaking with a sincere and humble heart. My mouth shall speak Your praise, and my whole being shall bless Your holy Name. Come, O Lord, do not tarry; relax the strict judgment that the sins of Your people deserve." Today St. Paul tells us in the Epistle that we are the dispensers of God's gifts, His mysteries. How near we must be to Him, and He to us! *Prope est.* It is almost whispered. He whom we have begged so insistently to come is very near, and darkness is dispersed, so that we may see our souls in His light.

In *Dominus* we see Him nearer to us; the *omnibus* spreads out to the whole world; and our voices here, invoking Him, reach up to heaven at *eum*. To all those who call upon Him with a sincere and humble heart, He comes down. But see how *veritate* lifts us back up to Him. So our response can be nothing else but praise: *laudem Domini* is a simple, direct answer, dropping in little groups of notes, softly, like gentle rain, because we still remember that He is "coming down," that the heavens will "show forth the glory of God." *Loquetur* seems to encourage us not to be afraid to let our song rise to Him, even though our voices in *os meum* seem to be like the prattle of little children.

A new idea, perhaps, comes in *et benedicat*: creatures of earth, daring to rise up to bless His holy Name! But it is not of our own accord—it is the psalmist counseling us to do so: Let all men bless the Lord! The music at *omnis caro* seems to favor the translation "all creatures" rather than "all flesh"—not

only earthlings, but God's creatures of the sky, far and wide. The
Holy Name societies should study the sweetness of that *nomen
sanctum ejus*. This Gradual is also a fine foreign-mission prayer:
May the mouth of every creature in the world soon sing Your
praises and bless Your holy Name, O Lord, God of nations!
Alleluia!

Veni is almost shy, perhaps because we have to reach up
and ask *Domine* in heaven to come. Once we are about our task,
though, we are emboldened to add, "and do not tarry!" Then
our next request, which continues in the clouds, soon comes
down to earth on the last syllable of *relaxa*, because it is from
our earthly offenses that we want Him to set us free. *Facinora* is
a much stronger word than *peccata* (*cf.* "malefactions" and "pec-
cadillos"). How is it possible for us to sing of our *facinora* to
such great heights? It is because we know that despite the fact
that they were so many and so great, and went on and on, they
were forgiven by His coming down to earth to redeem us. And
we are His people (*plebis tuae*), high and low, of all stations of
life, a people spreading out from one end of the earth to the
other. Another reason why we just have to add *Alleluia* again!

OFFERTORY – Luke 1:28,42.

This *Ave Maria* reminds us once more of the great place
our Lady has in the whole Advent liturgy. Even the poorest
mothers in the world make great sacrifices to provide joyful
Christmas feasts for their little ones; they are only imitating
Mary, who did so much to make Christmas possible for us. That
is why our voices soar to the greatest heights today in hailing
her and saying: "We thank you, Virgin Mother, for what you
have done for us. When Gabriel said his *Ave!* you thought not
of yourself, but of us, your children. We can never thank you
enough."

This *Ave* is perhaps one of the most beautiful of plain-chant
melodies. Note the loftiness of it throughout. The heights are
reached at *benedicta tu*. Note the new approach at *et benedictus*,
and the humility in *fructus ventris*. The repetition of *gratia plena*
at the words *ventris tui* emphasizes the truth that graces come to
us through Mary: "All to Jesus through Mary; all from Jesus
through Mary."

COMMUNION – Isaias 7:14.

"Just stop and notice this: a virgin shall conceive and give birth to a son, and his name shall be God-with-us." This chant seems to be filled with awe: that a virgin shall remain a virgin, and yet become a mother! The music of *Ecce* seems to say more, "Just stop and notice this," rather than the usual "Behold." Then *pariet* and *filium* reach up into heaven, indicative of the truth that all this is being accomplished by God's will.

The music of *et vocabitur Emmanuel* shows us how great is the name of "God-with-us." We understand this a little more clearly, perhaps, since He has just come to us in holy Communion. How truly He is with us! Our Lady could not keep Him with her always; but we can keep Him with us. May our song ever rise in awesome gratitude to our Emmanuel and His Mother!

MIDNIGHT MASS FOR CHRISTMAS

INTROIT – Psalm 2:7,1.

The first thing that strikes us as we look at the music of the Introit is its utter simplicity. Commercial interests have so robbed Christmas of that holyday's inherent beauty that we are almost disappointed to find the composer so sparing with his music for this great occasion. Evidently he was not concerned with gilding the lily; rather, he knew the mind of God. While *Dominus dixit ad me* looks like very simple music (and it is), just notice the majesty in it, the evenness—no fuss, no excitement. It is majestically calm, as if to say, "Here is a very simple statement, but so full of import for all men that it cannot be obscured." It is full of the simplicity of the manger.

Note how the same simple strain is repeated on *ego hodie*, telling us, "It is I, the Lord, who today gives you My Son." The words that follow are not so incongruous as one might at first imagine. They are a sigh from the eternal Father: "Although I this day give My Son to you, I know that there will be many who will not receive Him; that there will be some who will rage against Him, and others who, in their inane thoughts, will contra-

dict Him." Thank God, we are not of them! We have heard and
believed *Dominus dixit*, and in thanksgiving we reiterate it to the
whole world.

GRADUAL – Psalm 109:3,1.

Here the eternal Father continues the thought of the Introit:
"From the womb before the day-star, I have brought You forth,
My Son. I have given You power to rule souls; in the lives of
the saints, by the grace You will supply, great heights shall be
reached." Then we apply the words to ourselves, and say: "O
Lord, You have said to my soul, designed by You to be the
master and lord of my whole being: 'Sit at my right hand'; that
is, 'Be constant in good, and I will make your enemies of the
flesh and the evil one subject to you.' "

And this, again, through the grace brought to us by God's
Son. There is great dignity in the *tecum principium*, which rises
to superb heights because on this day is made manifest the power
of God: *in die virtutis tuae*. See the splendor of the saints reaching up to God while they are still on earth, a reflection of His
own great glory. *Ex utero* denotes great awe: one star, amid all
the stars in heaven, sending down a light, drawing us to the spot
where the Bud of eternal life shall rise from the ground.

Compare the simplicity of *Dixit Dominus Domino* to the
words at the beginning of the Introit. The majesty in it! The
meo soars because of the part that concerns me. The King of
kings speaks to me! The very thought lifts me to heaven, where
He hopes I may be always content to abide. "Be constant in
good" is an apt translation of *Sede*... while *scabellum pedum
tuorum* is sung to the same music as *ante luciferum genui te*, a
beautiful strain. There is a possible parallel: He whose birth is
signified by the day-star will give you all the help you need to
overcome the enemies of your soul.

ALLELUIA – Psalm 2:7.

If this seems familiar, look back to the Alleluia for the first
Sunday of Advent. On that Sunday we were pleading with God
to show us His mercy. Today's Alleluia is the answer: "Here is
My mercy; here is My only-begotten Son. See, I am sending Him
down from heaven for you today. I want Him to be known to

the very ends of the earth." Our Alleluia today, in its repetition, has something of the quality of a fervent *Deo gratias*.

OFFERTORY — Psalm 95:11,13.

"Let angels rejoice; let men be glad before the face of the Lord, who has come to us." Again St. Gregory does not have our rejoicing reach great heights; here is a quiet, restrained rejoicing. We cannot compete with the angels on this midnight— we must not try to do so. God is receiving the honor of all the choirs of heaven, and we are still "a little less than the angels." The music of *Laetentur* seems to say, "Let us reach up in our joy to the heavens (*coeli*) to achieve some of that joy while we are still down below on *terra*." *Ante* looks like a graceful curtsy or bow before the *faciem Domini*, who seems to look down from heaven at *venit*. It is very quiet and respectful, perhaps so as not to interfere with the offering being made at the altar.

COMMUNION — Psalm 109:3.

Here we have once more the words of the Gradual psalm. Here the eternal Father is speaking. Note the calm majesty of His voice. We have just received holy Communion; hence, the Father says to us: "The saints, by My grace and by much effort, have overcome themselves and their passions. Now you can do the same, for you are born by having My divine Son come into your hearts. *Luciferum genui te*—the Light of ages comes down to take up His abode with you. The peace of heaven is in that music. May it ever be in our hearts each day, as Christmas is re-enacted upon our altars. *Pax hominibus bonae voluntatis*: Peace to all those who are one in will with God.

THE THIRD MASS FOR CHRISTMAS

INTROIT — Isaias 9:6; Psalm 97:1.

"A Child is born for us, and a Son is given to us..."—the Boy Jesus, Son of God. Compare the somber music of the midnight Mass with this light, cheerful melody. How childlike this is! *Puer* is like the trumpet call we have met in other instances, like the stern order on naval vessels: "Now hear this!" As if to keep our attention, the music of *Puer natus est* is repeated at *et filius datus.* See how His empire (*imperium*) reaches up into heaven: "My kingdom is not of this world."

How easily it sets upon His shoulders in *super humerum ejus.* There is a great dignity throughout that phrase, as *cujus* begins at the hem of the robe that hangs from the King's shoulders, and *ejus* completes it. Again, we cannot help noting how tenderly His name is told. *Magni* is truly great; *consilii* testifies to the careful teaching with which He will surround us; *angelus*—between God and man. So, lightly and with great joy we announce to the world that we are singing a song to the Babe who, though but newborn, is doing such wonderful things for us.

GRADUAL — Psalm 97:3-4,2.

Abbot Smith's paraphrase is very apt in this instance: "Eternal Father, all the earth has seen Your beauty in the life of Your divine Son. Grant that all the earth may one day have our joy in You, and sing praise to You! You have clearly shown us Your salvation, because You have shown to all nations the beautiful life of Your Son." This Gradual continues one feature we noted in the Introit: an almost childlike repetition in the music, a repetition of awe and wonder and surprise.

No wonder we are surprised, for this Infant is not born for us alone: one day all peoples, all nations shall come to know that our God has come to bring them all safely home to heaven. That is why all the ends of the earth should join with us in singing praise to God. *Viderunt*—look and see, *omnes fines terrae.* Listen to the beauty in that saving grace of *salutare*; and again of *Dei*, who, though born on earth, belongs to heaven. The *nostri* shows His deep concern in having come down to us. See the simplicity of *jubilate*; would that all our joys were as simple and as sincere, in *Deo*, reaching up only to Him and content in having Him alone with us.

There is reverent wonder in the last seven notes of *omnis terra*; the music leaves us saying, "Ah, if only all men could know!" Note the childlike repetition of *fah, la, doh* on *omnis*, and again, one after the other, on *terra.* The Lord (*Dominus*) is He who has made known His saving grace to us. The frequent use of the same notes reaches a culmination towards the end of the word. It reminds us of what St. Paul says about our inability even to say the Name of the Lord unless we are empowered to do so by the Holy Spirit. Surely the music on *Dominus* is inspired! See the hope of lifting the Gentiles up to look upon His face in *gentium*; the truths made known to us of the earth in *revelavit*; and the calmness of His justice in *justitiam*.

ALLELUIA

The last notes echo the foregoing *salutare suum*, as if to point out one reason for offering this "song of praise to Him who is." *Dies* shows us a picture of the rising of the sun to its very setting; while *sanctificatus* is very holy. In *illuxit* we can see the Sun of eternal justice appearing over the horizon. He has come to en-lighten—*nobis*—and we can scarcely restrain ourselves. *Venite*: O come, all ye faithful, bow down before Him and lift up your eyes to see who He is, and then *adorate Dominum*! Notice once more how sacred is the Name of the Lord! Adore the Lord *hodie*, this glorious day of the Lord; and softly, now, we hear the reason: the Light of ages has descended, a Light so great that it reaches up from the earthly spot of His birth to shine on every-one and everything *super terram. Alleluia*: Sing songs of praise to Him who is!

OFFERTORY – Psalm 88:12,15.

"To You, eternal Father, belong the heavens and the earth; all the riches of the earth are Yours. You guide them whom You have chosen by holiness and prudence—virtues that make the hearts of men ready to be Your throne." One can see the applica-tion of the music at sight. Only one idea needs to be pointed out: the inspired composer would have us emphasize those two beauti-ful virtues of *justitiam et judicium*—let us say holiness and pru-dence. His throne (*sedes tuae*) is set up in our hearts, which keeps us above the earth and again just a little less than the angels.

COMMUNION – Psalm 97:3.

"All the earth has seen Your beauty, O my God, in the life of Your divine Son." While both the Gradual of today's Mass and the Communion have the same theme, their music differs. Both melodies are beautiful, but surely the shorter one, at the Communion, excels. The music on *terrae* and *salutare* is not so reserved as in other parts of the chant, because there is emphasis to be placed there, so that all may remember that "the earth and all the inhabitants of the earth have had salvation come to them."

The awe we feel at this announcement is expressed beautifully in *Dei nostri*; our God, who is ever ready to come into our hearts, is the same One who is the salvation of the whole world. We bow humbly, gratefully, under the promise given to us in the liturgy of this third Mass. But there must run all through these words the thread of prayer that will make it possible for all men, all over the world, to one day know that this message is as truly for them as it is for us, who are now privileged to participate in these mysteries.

SUNDAY AFTER CHRISTMAS

INTROIT — Wisdom 18:14-15; Psalm 92:1.

"While all things held the silence of midnight, Your almighty Word, O Lord, came quietly down to earth from the royal throne." This seems to sum up everything concerning Christmas that has not already been said. This passage from the Book of Wisdom refers to Israel's redemption from the rule and slavery of Egypt. In today's Mass the words have a new meaning: "While all the world lay wrapped in silence, God sent His only-begotten Son, the Word made flesh, into the world, that all men might thereby be redeemed from the slavery into which Adam's sin had cast them."

The whole Introit is, as it should be, a very solemn one, and each phrase is handled with great calmness and dignity. The first note shows us the depth from which we have been raised; the silence of the night wending its way is majestic, keeping our eyes and our voices above the earth, raising them to heaven, whence comes the *sermo omnipotens*. See us lifted up from *de caelis* and up to the royal throne (*regalibus sedibus*).

GRADUAL — Psalm 44:3,2.

"The beauty of Your soul, O Christ, my King, shall occupy my thoughts, and the grace You pour forth by Your words, so full of comfort, shall bring the eternal Father's blessing upon me. How can I say a good word when I am telling You of my own deeds? Only when You act with me, I may have good things to tell You. Then shall my lips be like the pen of a wise writer who limns his words swiftly; for only then shall I be able to tell of rapid progress in all virtues." One can almost hear this beautiful paraphrase by Abbot Smith sing itself!

Note the height to which *speciosus forma* rises, and how *filiis hominum*, though of the earth, are yet always straining toward heaven. How widely and generously *gratia* is *diffusa*. Would that our hearts, having once leaped up at God's good word, could have stayed up there with *cor meum* and *verbum bonum*! Unfortunately, the leap was a mistake; much better would have been a steady climb, for our brashness when we do try to put down our words for the King makes them come back tainted with earth. We sing the words, though, and we are not saddened by the memory of our failures; now we have learned how to keep our hearts, our thoughts, and our words close to the throne of the King, through the great boon He has granted us in coming down to us.

ALLELUIA — Psalm 92:1.

Hence, this verse takes on a newer, fuller meaning than it had when we chanted it on a psalm tone at the Introit this morning. The Lord has reigned, beautifully clothed. The Lord has robed Himself in fortitude and cinctured Himself with virtue, and the beauty of His apparel is made even more beautiful by the music. The thought of this picture of our Lord is continued in the

OFFERTORY — Psalm 92:1-2.

The music keeps the following prayerful thought on a very high plane: "O my Lord, set up Your kingdom in my heart, and ever clothe Yourself so beautifully in my sight that I may praise You with all the power that is given to me. Show Your strength, and subdue all the enemies of my soul. Let there be nothing in me that is not wholly subject to You. You have always been constant in Your love and care of me; keep me for Yourself forever."

COMMUNION — Matthew 2:20.

"Take the Child and His Mother, and go into the land of Israel, for those who sought the Child's life are now dead." We know that our redemption was to be bought with a great price, and so, before the Child was eight days old, we received some indication of the danger that was to come to Him. The Holy Family had been directed to hurry away into Egypt, away from those who would be sent to put the divine Child to death. How long the three Exiles remained in that foreign land we do not know, but we can well understand the anguish of our Lady and St. Joseph before they were bidden return to Israel.

Tolle seems to indicate the tender picking up of the Infant from His crib, that *Puerum* who is not of this world. Hear the tenderness in the music of *matrem ejus*; and see the wandering but hastening footsteps of *vade in terram Israel*. There is a rise in the song at the news that the persecutors are dead. But gradually the music returns to the earth, because Joseph and Mary must have known, as we know, that this was but one of the times when the Child's life would be sought. Enemies will arise again! But God, coming to us in holy Communion, will always give us the help we need to overcome our soul's enemies, if we but do our part well in each daily, Eucharistic visit. May we push forward to the promised land, away from the enemy, ever in the company of Jesus, Mary, and Joseph!

CIRCUMCISION OF OUR LORD

January 1

The proper of the Mass for today is taken almost entirely from the Third Mass at Christmas (see page 13). The only exception is to be found in the

ALLELUIA – Hebrews 1:1-2.

"In old days, God spoke to our fathers in many ways and by many means (fragmentarily and under various figures) through the prophets; now at last in these times He has spoken to us with a Son to speak for Him." The familiar Alleluia tone is repeated both in the first words, *multifarie olim*, and again, as usual, in the closing words, *in Filio suo*. This seems to draw our attention, first of all, to the lofty music of: "God spoke...through the prophets," where we can picture God, elevated above the earth, drawing the hearts and the minds of the prophets up to Himself in heaven.

What is more striking, however, is the emphasis which the music portrays in: "Now in these times He has spoken *to us!*" There is a fine spirit of joy in this music—and why not? God speaks directly to us through His divine Son. He tells us from the first that He is ready to shed His Blood for our redemption. *We* are the souls so dear to Him that our salvation is His prime concern. The idea humbles us, as it should, yet it rouses us to great rejoicing, since God has made known His salvation to us, and therefore "All the earth (should) sing joyfully to God." That is the true spirit of joy which should mark today's celebration.

EPIPHANY

This day might well be considered the first feast of Christ the King. The liturgy throughout the Divine Office and the Mass is concerned with the great dignity of Him who has appeared to us, of Him who, though revealing Himself as a Babe, has impressed upon us the royal character of His estate.

INTROIT — Malachias 3:1; Psalm 71:2.

This is most majestic; there are charm and grace in it throughout. Notice *Ecce*, like a trumpet calling our attention: "Here comes the Ruler, the Lord" (*advenit Dominus dominator*). There are other places in the liturgy and chant where these five notes serve as introduction to the coming of the Lord. In *advenit* one can almost hear the tread of pageantry approaching. "And the kingdom is in His hand" (*regnum in manu ejus*). Note the simplicity of *dominator, et regnum, et potestas*, and the majesty in the three phrases that follow each of these. *Dominus* is repeated almost exactly in *imperium*, emphasizing the empire, the dominion of the Lord.

During the four weeks of Advent we pleaded, "Come, Lord, and do not tarry"; today the Lord answers our prayer, coming to establish His kingdom in our hearts. He brings *potestas*, the power that will make us children of God and heirs of heaven. Yes, the Introit has great majesty; and part of that belongs to us, too, through His coming.

GRADUAL – Isaias 60:6,1.

This is really a repetition of the words of Isaias read in the Epistle; and the Gospel that follows seems to say: "What Isaias promised actually came to pass." What a profound impression that should make upon us! Note *omnes*—all people, both those of high station and those of low; and in *de Saba venient* one can almost see the caravan coming. *Aurum* and *thus* are things above this earth, the gold of heavenly grace and the incense of prayer risen to heaven; while *deferentes* shows the dispensing action of the Kings. Notice how simply the music of *et laudem Domino* expresses the idea of praise to the Lord—direct, clear, unadorned, wholesome, and pure. The voice of such praise should be as widespread as is the music of *annuntiantes*.

At *Surge* we hear the courtier's trumpet that bade the people to stand up when their king was approaching; and at *illuminare* we can see the torches being lighted, rising from the tiniest spark to a great flame. *Jerusalem* has fallen from its former high estate, yet it rises again to great heights at *Domini*: the glory of the Lord has risen over us, who are now the privileged children of a heavenly Jerusalem. In olden days, when city illumination was unknown, great flares and torches were lighted along the king's way for two reasons: so that no one would have opportunity under the cover of darkness to do harm to the king; and so that, by the light of the torches, His Majesty could plainly see the faces of all his subjects. May our King's grace, shining on our upturned faces, show Him that our hearts, too, are truly lifted up to Him!

ALLELUIA – Matthew 2:2.

After the glorious opening we hear the song of the three Wise Men: "We have seen His star in the East, and have come to adore Him." *Vidimus* seems to picture: "We saw a star, and we began to follow it as it moved through the heavens." Note the simplicity of *stellam*, the star of Him who dwelt in heaven but deigned to come down to earth to us. The Wise Men's story might continue: "In the Orient, where the sun first appears above the horizon, we came to realize that the Sun of eternal justice was bidding us to rise and come (*venimus*) to Him. So we gathered the most excellent gifts (*muneribus*) and brought them to lay at His feet, while we lift our heads and hearts and hands to adore Him (*adorare*), the Lord of heaven and earth (*Dominum*)."

OFFERTORY – Psalm 71:10-11.

In direct address, the thoughts can be expressed as follows: "All nations shall put themselves willingly under Your dominion, O God, and shall bring costly presents to You. The kings of the earth shall gladly adore You, and all nations shall do as You bid them." The music begins with the dignity that is attendant upon royalty; then the music of *munera offerent*, rising and receding, portrays the act of offering gifts. One can almost see the dromedaries of *Arabum et Saba*! As with *munera offerunt, donna adducent* expresses the act of giving, but perhaps with higher motives. See the adoration of the Kings falling down (*adorabunt eum*) and note the parallel in both *munera offerent* and *servient ei*. All their gifts were nothing else but their outward expression of the little catechism lesson: having known, they came to love and to serve.

COMMUNION – Matthew 2:2.

"We have seen His star in the East and have come with gifts to adore the Lord." These same words were sung in the Alleluia verse, and the music here adequately emphasizes the same lofty ideas. Yet they also pose a question based on the words of our consideration of the Offertory above: "Now that you have received the Giver of all good gifts in holy Communion, what gifts have you to offer Him? You know Him in the Bread of Angels. What will be your evidence of loving service?" Our answer: "Only gifts of love—love of souls, love of all mankind, love of God's interests, love of His holy will, love of the God of love—*cum muneribus* only *adorare Dominum*!"

FEAST OF THE HOLY FAMILY

(Sunday within the Octave of Epiphany)

INTROIT – Proverbs 23:24-25; Psalm 83:2,3.

"Rejoice with great joy, O Father of the Just One; and you, O Mother who bore Him, exult with gladness. O my Lord, I will strive to appreciate the beauty of the life to which You have called me. Your home is, indeed, full of delight and beauty. Let me learn from my life here to long for Your house, of which this is but the court." The music rises gently but powerfully up to the Father (*Pater justi*) and again at *Pater tuus*, the most high God; but see how gracefully it descends on *et Mater tua*, since His Mother was a creature of earth like ourselves. Because God chose her for so high a role in the incarnation, her joy (*exultet*) is of heaven, too, whence, the Just One came to be born (*genuit*) on earth.

The word *tabernaculum* in the psalm verse reminds us that Mary was the first tabernacle of Christ. But now we have Him not only in the tabernacle on our altar, but in each one of us who becomes a living tabernacle after He is "born" again on our altar and comes into our hearts in holy Communion. The Introit should be sung joyfully, but I have noticed that the choir always seems to find difficulty in correctly singing the phrase *et Mater tua*. I have recommended that those three words be sung a little more slowly and softly; it helps to get the proper rendition. Then let the choir continue rejoicing with *et exsultet*.

GRADUAL – Psalm 26:4; Psalm 83:5.

"One thing I beg very earnestly from You, O Lord: that You will let me dwell near You all my life. Blessed are they who in this life find their home where You dwell, and where they may begin even here the work of praise that is to occupy them for ever and ever." The melody is a simple one and similar to others we have been singing. The music of the first two words says, in effect, "I have but a simple request to which I wish You would bend Your ear, O God." But then, as the voice reaches up to God on *Domino*, it becomes more courageous. *Inhabitem in domo Domini* gives us something of the picture of the Negro spiritual, "walking all over God's heaven"; and *omnibus diebus vitae meae* portrays the idea of "as many months and years as my life shall last." There is a slight change in the melody that follows, but it retains the simplicity of the former verses, except for *Domine* and *laudabunt te*, as though we hope never to end the praise of God even on earth.

ALLELUIA – Isaias 45:15.

"Truly You are a hidden King, O God of Israel, our Savior." This is familiar, but note the solemnity of *vere* and the gradual approach through *tu es* to the words that follow. *Deus Israel* is a strong song of faith; and in *Salvator* we see the picture of our Lord showing Himself as the Savior of all men, all nations, everywhere. May this beautiful song be our prayer that He will not remain hidden and unknown to those in the world who need Him urgently!

OFFERTORY – Luke 2:22.

"The parents of Jesus took Him up to Jerusalem, to present Him to the Lord." Before you sing the words, sing the melody alone and see if it is not familiar. Yes, it is the same music as at the Offertory of the Christmas midnight Mass. In today's Offertory the music of *tulerunt* shows us our Lady and St. Joseph leading the Infant toward the holy City. The music for the word *Jesum* is reverent with great beauty. The notes on the word *Jerusalem* give something of a picture of the minarets of the Temple there, and *sisterunt* presents a picture of offering. There may have been no connection in the mind of those who applied this melody to today's Offertory, but it seems to me a parallel: the angels who were bidden to rejoice at His coming at midnight are rejoicing again today as He is presented by His parents in the Temple. If we can imagine with what joy Mary and Joseph made their offertory, we can be united with them in ours today as we sing this familiar strain.

COMMUNION – Luke 2:51.

"Jesus went down with His parents on their journey to Nazareth, and lived there in subjection to them." The music of *descendit* is truly a picture in itself, and that of *Jesum* is very reverent. To me, the music of *cum eis* presents the picture of a child holding onto his parents' hands as he walks along with them. When the Holy Family neared their home city, their hearts must have swelled with relief and happiness, as *et venit Nazareth* seems to indicate.

There He, the God who came down from heaven was subject to them in all humility (*subditus illis*). How beautifully the music presents this picture! As we marvel at it, we might ask this same Jesus, now with us through holy Communion, to teach us the lesson of subjecting ourselves to Him through our superiors. He will probably repeat, *"Exemplum dedi vobis...."* May we never depart from any phase of that glorious example!

SECOND SUNDAY AFTER EPIPHANY

INTROIT – Psalm 65:4,1-2.

"Let the whole earth adore You, O God, singing Your holy Name. I will sing joyfully to You, O God, with all the earth. I will praise You with the words of the psalms, and glorify Your holy Name." These two verses express one and the same idea, but the second verse, used as the psalm, seems to emphasize the thought. The whole Introit is one beautiful paean of joy from beginning to end, and the music gives happier meaning to the words.

Omnis terra lifts its voice up from the earth and then seems to fall in adoration before God. Note the ascending *te* and the majestic awe in the music of *Deus*. We are singing the psalms, not for the joy we get therefrom, but because those inspired songs lift us surely toward heaven. Notice *nomini*—"the name that came from heaven and belongs to all that is heaven." This is made clearer for us by the beautiful tones of *tuo*, and the majesty of *Altissime*. Dom Johner says: "Every nation ought to adore God, to sing to His name, and all the earth should glorify Him. We know how little this admonition is heeded. This ought to awake in us the resolution to sing this song with so much more reverence and joy."[1]

[1] *op. cit.*, p. 88.

In the Epistle of today's Mass, St. Paul bids us to be ever on God's side. Some of God's friends suffered many things for Him rather than lose His friendship. How God dealt with those friends is told in the

GRADUAL — Psalm 106:20-21.

"But You did heal them with the word of Your mouth, and You snatched them from destruction. May Your mercies give glory to You, O God; and may Your wonderful works to the children of men also glorify You! Give me courage to praise You in company with the angels, to praise You in company with those spirits that do Your will on earth."

The words alone provide a wealth of material for meditation; but set to music, they lift us to great heights. See how God leans down at *Dominus* to send us assurance of His Word, the *Verbum* that came down from heaven to earth. There is balm for men's souls in the music of *sanavit*, lifting them (*eos*) from the depths of their trials to the greatest heights, snatching them from destruction. Notice the simplicity of *eripuit*. It is not difficult for God to "snatch" us away from danger when we keep ourselves close by, ready to take His extended hand. The notes at the end of *eorum* have a healing comfort in them.

In *confiteantur* we have an idea of the stubborn insistence of men confessing God's mercies. The unusual repetition here seems to say: "We repeat, again and again: God has shown great mercies to us, mercies (*misericordiae*) that reached down to us in our lowest estate and lifted us high above the earth. Even when we fell away, it was His mercy that moved Him to lift us up again and again." There is great awe in the *mirabile* that the *filiis hominum* are thereby enabled to render glory to God because of the mercy He has shown.

ALLELUIA — Psalm 148:2.

This is the very joyful melody that we met on the third Sunday of Advent. (We shall hear it again on Ascension Day, and then once more on Pentecost.) The same music that anticipated the coming of the Lord seems to show us how to praise Him with a joyful song in our hearts.

OFFERTORY — Psalm 65:1-2,16.

"I will sing joyfully to You, O God, with all the earth. I repeat it: my song will be one with all the earth. I will give all glory to Your Name as I sing songs of the wonderful things You have done, and I will invite all who fear You, all who do not yet know love, to come and hear what great things You have done for my poor soul."

Repetition in both the words and the music of an Offertory is a rare occurrence. This one is so much a song of joy—one of the greatest in the music of the Church—that the mere singing of it once did not seem to satisfy the jubilant soul of the composer. The first *Jubilate* is the clarion call of the trumpet. The second is like saying: "I must come down from heaven, where all rejoicing should be centered, and lead men step by step to the heights—one step more, now another"—until we are at the pinnacle of rejoicing, with a glorious song of praise. Note the extent of *universa terra*, the heights and depths, far and wide; note the great awe and reverence in *nomine ejus*. St. Gregory surely had a deep love for God's Name; this is evident in the music every time we meet *nomen ejus* or *nomen Domini*.

The music on *venite et audite* is very interesting. One can visualize the man standing atop the mount of joy and beckoning with all the strength of his arms, as he calls to all men in the valley below: "Come and listen to me, and I will tell you wonderful things!" *Omnes* stretches out to all; and *qui timet* seems a little pitying, because *Deus* is calm, kind, loving and should not be feared. See the great things coming down from heaven in *quanta fecit*: God, reaching down from heaven to my poor soul! The *Alleluia* at the close seems to be a natural outburst of joy, bringing to a happy conclusion a beautiful, jubilant hymn.

(There are few chant melodies that cover such a range from C to G, as does this Offertory. If it is sung in the key of C, the highest note will be F, which can easily be glanced off the three times it appears. A lower key would rob the melody of its inherent joy.)

COMMUNION — John 2:7-9,10-11.

The Gospel story is condensed for us here in a most unusual melody. Note the simplicity of *Dicit*, but the majesty of *Dominus*.

Then the music of the next six words is very expressive. It even seems like the tones of a person talking very calmly but firmly, emphasizing his words so that they may be correctly understood: "Fill up—the jars—with water—and take—to the steward." The next words are set to a very matter-of-fact kind of music until we reach the word *dicit*; then the steward seems to chide the bridegroom: "You've kept the good wine until now!" There is almost a smacking of lips on *bonum*, and a glad excitement seems to follow.

If the composer had a sense of humor—and it seems he did—he knew when to be serious, too. Hear the sober dignity in the words that follow: "This was the first sign that Jesus worked in the presence of His disciples." The last notes of the music seem scarcely to end because, as we know, it was not the last sign. Perhaps, too, it was so given to us that we might think of the other great sign that has just been enacted before our eyes in the holy Sacrifice, the unending mystery of God changing bread and wine into His own Body and Blood, and of our participation in the Sacrifice, the unsearchable mystery of His having made us members of His Mystical Body, the Church. *Hoc signum fecit Jesus.*

THIRD SUNDAY AFTER EPIPHANY

The proper of the Mass for this Sunday remains the same for the three Sundays that sometimes follow now, or that fill in the Sundays after Pentecost when Easter comes early in the year.

INTROIT – Psalm 96:7-8,1.

Adorate is the imperative form of the verb, but we could make this Introit song more of a prayer than a command by adapting it: "May Your holy angels, whom You have chosen to be Your messengers, adore and praise You, O God. May Your Church (*Sion*) hear and rejoice in the honor given to you. May the daughters of Jerusalem, the chosen souls of Your Church, be glad because of the mercy of Your rule, O my God. — Your kindly rule makes the whole world rejoice; even the islands afar off shall be glad."

The music of the first word, *Adorate*, is almost severe; but after that we notice the ascent and descent of the adoring angels. The notes remind us throughout of the errands of angels between God and men. The strongest evidence of this is on *filiae Judae*—a sweeping down and up, and then down again. The beautiful picture of the angels shows us, too, how active they are from the very beginning of the holy Sacrifice. They are ready to lift us to heaven with them, to keep our hearts close to the throne all during this majestic Oblation. And so, in imitation of them, we bow in adoration, praying that all the people of the world, the people of the islands afar off, may one day bow with us. This Introit should be a fervent mission prayer.

Since we are aware of our own weakness, in the Collect we ask God to extend His right hand and lift us up to Him, so that with Him we may be protected from falling into the wrong frame of mind that St. Paul condemns in the Epistle. Then the reason for our prayer seems to be contained in the

GRADUAL – Psalm 101:16-17.

Again, an adaptation may be helpful! "Your kindness to me will make those who forget You have reverence for You, O Lord; and the rulers of darkness, the evil spirits, will acknowledge Your glory. For You are the Creator of my soul, and You have made it for Your own glory." The music on *timebunt* is strong, firm, making *gentes* fall and cower before the glory of *nomen tuum*. Note again what we remarked last week and what will often appear: the beauty and sweetness of the music whenever God's Name is mentioned; also the majestic melody of *Domine*. Let one sing those three words alone, *nomen tuum, Domine*, and hear the reverence of that melody.

Then the music seems to indicate that if nations will but give the example of glorifying God's Name, then the kings of the earth will be lifted up above their realms to eternal heights, giving glory to God. See the repetition of the first three notes on *gloriam*, and the awe of that word. The very music seems to emphasize what we saw on New Year's Eve: that God's glory is, intrinsically, His own perfections. How simple the music is on *quoniam* but how immediately *aedificavit* builds up to the glory of God's Church (*Dominus Sion*). *Et videbitur*—this majesty must be plainly seen by others, existing in all of us who comprise His Church. *Dominus* calmly in heaven *regnavit*; and we catch another glimpse of the angels hovering around His throne. In *exultet* the joy of heaven is brought to *terra*. The joy (*laetentur*) is as extensive as the effort made to bring the far-flung islands to the knowledge and love of God.

OFFERTORY – Psalm 117:16-17.

This is like an answer to our Collect prayer: "Take me by the right hand, O my God, and raise my soul to You. In Your strength I shall be saved from (eternal) death, and my soul, living with Your life, shall praise You and show to others the goodness You have shown to me." This Offertory is taken from the Holy Thursday Mass, and we can imagine why that has been done: we pray today that God's hand may sustain us; the Gospel tells us that His hand was extended to the leper who was thereby made clean; the leprosy of sin will be cleansed by His hand. So on Holy Thursday, Christ may use the fulfillment words for Himself.

In our Offertory, when we are able to offer to God all that we have and are, it will be complete renunciation. Yet we shall not die; but through our part in the holy Sacrifice we shall receive new life in our souls, a life that we cannot hide but must make known to others, so that they may see how wonderfully God works through us when we make ourselves one with Him. *Dextera* shows strength, and in *Domini* we see the Lord stooping down to give us the strength of heaven (*virtute*). His heavenly hand exalts me so that not death but the life of heaven shall be in me (*non moriar sed vivam*). Then I shall lift up my voice from the earth and tell (*narrabo*) of all His works (*opera Domini*), which speak, too, of His glory.

COMMUNION – Luke 4:22.

This verse might have followed the portion of St. Matthew's Gospel read in today's Mass. "All were astonished at the gracious words which came from His mouth" is from St. Luke, but those words might easily have been recorded in connection with today's events. See the wide-eyed astonishment in *mirabantur*. It is a very pleasant form of surprise, not one of shock. Those things (*de his*) that our Lord made known were things of heaven. See them falling from God's lips down to us in *de ore,* and hear the calm gratitude in the music of *Dei.*

When God deigns to let fall into our souls not only His words but also Himself, Body and Blood, soul and divinity, may our gratitude bespeak our constant surprise that we are so favored among the people of God's earth! May those favors move us, too, to pray for the other sheep who are not yet of this fold, in lands afar as well as in places nearby! Adore Him with the angels; reach out to the islands afar off with His grace. His right hand sustains you; He is with you. For three more Sundays we are to be strengthened with these thoughts, so that when Septuagesima comes we may face with great courage and greater love the penitential season that follows.

SEPTUAGESIMA

INTROIT — Psalm 17:5-7,2-3.

"The dangers that accompany me, O God, are very many: there is the danger of sin, which would be the death of my soul; there is the fierce torment of my passions; there are temptations of hell all about me, seeking to shake my trust in You; and there are incitements to pleasure, to ensnare me if I am not on my guard. In all my troubles and dangers, I will call upon You; I will continue to beseech You not to abandon me, O my God!— My love shall be fixed on You, my God, for You are my only strength, enabling me to persevere in the vocation You have given me. You surround me as a firmament; You are my refuge in all the trials of life, and my protection in all temptation."

Yesterday at Vespers we bade farewell to the *Alleluia* until Holy Saturday night; and with that cessation, joy seems to have gone. The music of today's liturgy verifies this fact in every instance. There are only a few places in the Introit where the voice rises to any considerable height: one is when we call on the Lord—*invocavi Dominum, et exaudivit;* another on the second *circumdederunt;* and then on *dolores.* Hear the *dolor* in that word! Since Christmas Eve we have been singing gay, almost lilting melodies, but now there is restraint.

GRADUAL – Psalm 9:10-11,19-20.

"You are my Helper, O God, in all my needs. I will trust You, for You have shown Your kindness to me, allowing me to call You mine. Seeking, let me always find You, O Lord. Since I am poor and needy, You will not forget me. Give me patience to wait Your time and trust You to the last. Arise, O Lord, and let no human nature prevail in me."

It would be good for us to recall these words in any physical suffering that may become ours. And since they are suggestive, too, of all who suffer bodily ills, perhaps we could make this Gradual a prayer today for the sick and infirm. On *Adjutor* note how the voice reaches up to heaven, calling for help. Our trials on earth (*in tribulatione*) are of the earth, but our cry for help will pierce the skies. Notice how the music points to the continual struggle between the soul and the body: the soul straining towards heaven, where it wants to stay, and the body continually dragging us back to earth. Once more, there is sheer beauty in the music of *Domine*. Then the struggle goes on and is most graphically shown on the word *homo*. Note how the poor in spirit (*pauperum*), the patient lowly ones, are lifted to the greatest heights. It seems an echo from the *Magnificat*: "He has filled the needy with good things, and has sent the rich away, empty."

TRACT – Psalm 129:1-4.

The *De Profundis* should not need a translation, but Abbot Smith's paraphrase is so fine, it will appear almost like a new prayer: "Out of the depths of my own selfishness, I have cried to You, O my God; listen to me, please, and be ever attentive to me, O Lord. Ah, how little need there has been in the past to attend to my cry, for I have not called to You! I did not look to You for help. Attend to me doubly, now, that I may turn to You. I have delayed too long. Wait for me now a little, O Lord; I am so slow. I know You are all mercy; I need much mercy and much forgiveness. O Lord, my God, I shall await Your time; only make me constant."

Because we cry from the depths, our song here does not reach the heights it did in the Gradual, yet there is the constant surge of the soul trying to lift itself up. Hear the piercing cry in *clamavi* and the lingering on the first *Domine*, especially the repetition of the six notes at the beginning of the second line. There is prayerfulness in the music of *orationem*. Notice how little singing there is on *iniquitates*, pointing out to us that we should not dwell on our sins, but rather admit that we have been unprofitable servants who have neglected our duty to love. Note the cry of love in *Domine*.

OFFERTORY – Psalm 91:2.

"It is true that I forgot You, O my God; but now I come to offer You all that I have, all that I am, and I do it joyfully. I know it is not much: a weak will, a heart slow to love, too much of self—yes, I confess that. It is good to confess to the Lord."

This melody is a little more cheerful, indicative of what is now possible for us. *Bonum est*: it is good for me to lift my voice to heaven to sing (*psallere*) the beauty of God's most holy Name (*nomini tuo*). Note how "most high" is shown in the music of *altissime*. We are privileged, in each Offertory, to unite our poor offering with the great oblation of our Head. His manifold attributes and virtues will absorb our petty gifts; and they, united with His, will take on great value in the eyes of the most high God.

COMMUNION – Psalm 30:17-18.

There is a quiet, hushed awe about this. We have made our poor offering, and for it we have received in return all that heaven contains! The words of the psalm form a beautiful prayer: "Let the light of Your face shine upon Your servant, O Lord, and be ever merciful to me. Let me never be put to shame when I call upon You!" The first part of this chant is very prayerful; note the reverent music of *faciem tuam* and the humility of *super servum tuum*. Then the hope of the prayer being answered is indicated in the reaching tones of *in tua*.

The same music of *misericordia* and *Domine non* unite the two thoughts: "God's mercy is lasting. How greatly it differs from the mercy we may look for in this world!" We have offered ourselves, our nothingness, to God; He has given us Himself, our All. Why? Each favored soul can say, *Quoniam invocavi te*—"Because I have called upon You."

SEXAGESIMA

INTROIT — Psalm 43:23-26,2.

"Arise, O Lord, and be as if You are no longer asleep to me and have no care of me. In Your mercy, leave me not to despair; turn not Your face away from me. You know my utter need of You, O Lord. The story of Your mercy and kindness to souls is constantly told to us."

The music of *Exsurge* this time is not the call of the trumpet, but rather a gentle pleading: "Don't You think You ought to listen to me?" Hear, too, how questioning the music is in the next three words. Say aloud, "Why do You pretend to sleep?"— and then hear it in the very notes! The next *Exsurge* is a little higher, still pleading. And it continues almost apologetically, as if to say: "I know, O Lord, You have much cause to find me repellent to You. But if You will reign in my heart, I will so try to amend my life that You may not be similarly disposed to me at its end."

The *Quare* is something of a coaxing question; note the question mark in the music of *avertis* and in *oblivisceris*: "Have You forgotten our petty tribulations?" Then realizing that what we call trouble is nothing but the result of our own selfish temporal affairs, the music drops to earth at that. It quickly rises like a trumpet call on the third *exsurge*, because we realize that if God makes haste and rises to help us and free us, we shall be able to lift ourselves up by His grace, and our ears (*auribus nostris*) shall once more hear His heavenly words.

GRADUAL — Psalm 82:19,14.

"The enemies of our peace, the enemies of our souls one day shall know that You are their God, and that You are the most high, against whom none can stand. My God, make their advice unstable, like a turning wheel that is loose; and make their fury like chaff before the wind.

In the Epistle today, St. Paul tells us that only God's grace can overcome the enemies of our soul. The same thought is carried over into the Gradual. *Sciant gentes* is like a gentle threat; yes, the Gentiles shall one day know, because the *Doctor gentium* will see to that. We, all Christians, are doctors to the Gentiles, to those who do not yet know the true God's Name. Hear how beautiful that passage of music is, how it rises to heaven, and how *Deus* is a repetition of *nomen tibi*. The Gentiles must learn that God only is most high; and the music pierces the heavens briefly, only to come back to earth to show us how much higher He is than we. This same musical thought is repeated in *super omnem terram*: not only above us, but above all creatures over the world, many of whom are to hear of Him only through us. The *Deus* in the next verse is reverent, and the fact that we can say, "He is my God (*Deus meus*)" lifts us to heaven. See the un- stable, wobbly wheel in *rotam*, and the action of the wind (the Holy Spirit) blowing away the fury of our enemies like chaff.

TRACT – Psalm 59:4,6.

This continues the thought of the Gradual: "We have lis- tened to the enemies of our souls, O Lord; and because of that, You have permitted commotions of the earth, letting it be troubled with earthquakes. But now, close the fissures that we may stand on solid ground. Our safety is in flight, O Lord, if we would ever remain Your beloved, that is, remain and grow in grace."

These words alone could provide a fine meditation for to- day. Think of them as you look at the music of *Commovisti*, *conturbasti*, and *mota est*, portraying earthquakes. The remedy (*Sana*) is to be found only in heavenly grace coming down to those who are sorry for the havoc that sin has wrought. There is great determination in the music of *fugiant....* We know what we must do to enjoy the sweetness of *liberentur*, we who have freely chosen Christ as the love of our souls.

OFFERTORY – Psalm 16:5,6-7.

This reminds us of the parable just sung in the Gospel, that of the various seeds sown in the earth. And so, as we offer our- selves to God in the holy Sacrifice, we pray that we may grow to perfection, if He will bend down in His mercy to us, for He is our only hope, our firm trust. The music seems to emphasize these three points of our prayer, too. Note the new trend in *in- clina* and again at *mirifica*. Notice how *semitis* leads directly to God by the path that leads to Him; and the firmness in the mu-

sic of *non moveantur vestigia mea*—"that I shall not suffer my
footsteps to be diverted from His path." Again, *inclina* is a
graceful stooping down to *verba mea*, which try to reach God's
ear. There is awe in the wonder of *misericordias*, and the peacefulness of hope in *sperantes*. Once more, listen to how sweetly
the composer sings the name of the Lord (*Domine*).

If this Offertory is not sung according to notation, the organist, instead of using some inept motet, could play this music
as an interlude. It should not be difficult to see the long line of
early Christians with their gifts approaching the altar in procession, singing this beautiful song along the way. We may even
have difficulty in keeping our own hearts from urging us to
march down the aisle!

COMMUNION – Psalm 42,4.

"My God, grant that I may not hesitate, but go in confident-
ly to Your holy place, trusting in You, who give me all the joy
of life."

This Communion prayer seems very apt. Since we have already offered ourselves, we should not have any fear or hesitation
about entering the holy precincts of the altar to receive the Lord
of heaven, for He is the God who has given true, lasting happiness
to our lives; He is the one who would have me always come as
a child. All the music of this song is very exalted. *Introibo* marches
right up and down again, only to return to the greatest heights
at *altare Dei*. Then *ad Deum* goes directly up to God, as it should;
and *laetificat* seems to laugh with the lighthearted joy of *juventu-
tem meam*. Today's liturgy is very much like the story of every
Christian's life. We pass through trials from the enemies of our
souls, but if we hold fast to the grace that is always given to us,
we shall one day enter into the joy and peace of unending union
with Him whose help is more than sufficient for us. So be it, O
Lord; may it, indeed, be so!

QUINQUAGESIMA

We are on the threshold of Lent; we plan today our preparation for that season of grace. In the Gospel our Lord tells His apostles of His coming sufferings. But they cannot understand. The eyes of faith are not yet fully opened for them; they are like the blind man at the side of the road. With that man we must cry, "Lord, that I may see!" St. Paul in his Epistle shows us that our faith and the seeing into our own souls must have a foundation of love. It is love that takes us into the refuge of God's Heart, where faith is increased through the nourishment that He will set before us.

INTROIT – Psalm 30:3-4,2.

The whole message of today's liturgy is contained in the psalm, which may be freely rendered: "In You, O God, my hope is fixed. Put me not to shame in the last day. You will free me from all my difficulties if I seek to follow Your most just will." Abbot Smith gives the following translation: "My God, be to me a Father and Protector. Be my refuge to which I may fly at all times; for my strength is from You, and if I seek refuge in any other, I shall certainly be deceived. You, my God, will nourish me and make me strong against the enemies of my soul."

There is a simple, childlike joy in this Introit. The first line sounds very much like a little child telling of a visit he is going to make to some relative's house. There are pride, assurance, and delight in the child's voice, because he knows that loving understanding awaits him. Hear the child saying in the next line, "It's *very nice* down there, and He is going to take care of me." The whole Introit carries the idea of naive joy. The greatest outburst is at *dux mihi eris*: "You will be my leader." Who wouldn't rejoice at being confident of what must follow from such leadership! The next word, *et*, lengthened as it is, sounds like the child again enumerating the good things he is going to get: "A-a-and ...He will give me food for my soul." There is no sadness in the child's heart: there is no sadness in preparing for Lent, but a joyful hope of the loving understanding that will come to us in that holy season.

GRADUAL – Psalm 76:15,16.

We sing of the same realization in the Gradual: "Who can do so much with my poor weak soul, O God, as You can? Your great power is known over the whole world. You showed Your might by taking a weak and despised people and raising them to do great things for You. I praise You for that!

The first word in the Latin, *Tu*, is very reverent, as is *Deus*. *Facis* is a little intricate, as if to indicate that the wonders God performs are not easy to do. See the great similarity in *virtutem* and *tuam*, and the strength of God's arm in *brachio*, which He exercises for His people (*populum tuum*) all over the world, and those scattered children of Israel. This Gradual and also the Tract that follows must be sung in a spirit of joyful confidence, in spirited rendition that does not lag. You will be able to see the reason for that from a mere glance at the music with its extensive neums in so many places. To drag them out would be painfully distracting to persons who have their thoughts on the Oblation.

TRACT – Psalm 99:1-2.

"The praise that I give You, my God, must be full of joy and con-*fide*-nce. Give me grace to serve You joyfully and with a generous heart. Let me enter into Your presence with no fear, but with the pleasure of intimacy, for I know that You are my Lord and God who loves me. You have made me; I have not made myself. Whatever I have is Your gracious gift."

The music of the Tract will sound familiar. The opening strain appears in other places where the invitation to joyful confidence is given. Just the word *Jubilate* alone is happy; note the reverence in the music of *Domino*; the music of *laetitia* is so happy that the *ti* almost sounds like children bubbling over at the opportunity of serving their Father. There is beautiful music in the word *Deus* that follows soon—God who made us to be His sheep that He might be our Shepherd. There is a familiar ring to *pascuae ejus*; it is music that is often heard when referring to the whole worldful of sheep under the eye of the loving Herdsman.

OFFERTORY – Psalm 118:12-13.

Abbot Smith's translation is as follows: "You are blessed, O Lord. Teach me more and more to know Your holy will in

my regard. I thank You for allowing me to spend my life in singing Your praise in the Divine Office." Like the Offertory for the
second Sunday after Epiphany, this one emphasizes the first part
by repeating not only the words but also the music.

The second time *tuas* is sung, it is at greater length; the first
tuas is like an abbreviation of the second. It would be an interesting attempt if the cantors alone sang the first *Benedictus*...
tuas, and the whole choir sang it the second time, as if to say,
"Yes, and teach us, too!" *Benedictus* is prayerful, and *Domine* is
very reverent. If we think of *justificationes* as God's will, it is easy
to see the import of the music, concerning things of heaven in our
regard. *In labiis meis*: may each of us, after being taught, let the
words that come from the lips be only such that will reach into
heaven, words of praise that may draw a favorable judgment for
us from God's mouth. Then like the blind man in the Gospel,
we begin "to see" God's will in our regard; faith and confidence
are rewarded, and we offer ourselves anew in union with our
Lord in the holy Sacrifice.

COMMUNION – Psalm 77:29-30.

"So the people had their wish and were filled with the food
of their choice. God did not stint them in the food they craved."
This follows beautifully upon our reception of holy Communion.
The music for the whole piece is restrained and prayerful. The
only rise above the normal is at *eis Dominus*, as if to impress
upon us that the Food, which is God, has been given to us by
God. The Communion sums up the message of today's liturgy:
by faith, keep your ears open to God's teaching, your eyes open
to see Him in all creatures, your heart open to love; and He will
satisfy all your needs by giving Himself as your strength, your
courage, your food, your reward exceeding great.

FIRST SUNDAY OF LENT

Because Psalm 90 is used throughout today's Mass, it would be well to quote here, in its entirety, Abbot Smith's paraphrase of this beautiful song. In the various parts of the Mass we shall find it easy, then, to refer to the verses that are to be sung.

PSALM 90

1. Happy is the man who trusts constantly in Your help, O Lord God most high, for he shall dwell at peace under Your protection.

2. I will speak to You, my Lord, for You are my protector, my fortress to whom I can fly; my God, in whom I will place all my trust.

3. You have rescued me from the snare of the evil one; he has striven to make me lose confidence in You and to trust in myself; he has sought to disturb me by the sharp criticism to which I have been exposed. But You, my good God, have taught me how to disregard these temptations.

4. You will screen me yet more from his attacks with Your strength. You will comfort me under Your wings.

5. Your truth will be to me a shield, giving me right principles whereby to repel the attacks of Satan. I will rely on You, my God, and not be cast down when I am assaulted in the night.

6. I will not fear for the attacks that come upon me openly, or those that assail my soul in secret; or for such as come upon me in the full glare of day.

7. A thousand who trust not in You, my God, may fall beside me, and ten thousand close to my right hand. But by Your protection, their fall shall not hurt me.

8. Their fall shall only be a warning to me, and I shall know what You will do to them for their sin.

9. For You, O Lord, are my hope; You the Most High are my refuge, my safe retreat.

10. No evil can harm me, and no trial can come upon me, save such as You in Your wisdom shall see is good for me.

11. You have given Your angels charge over me; they will keep me in all my ways, and will save me from harm.

12. They shall bear me up in their hands, lest I hurt my foot against a stone. O Lord, my God, how kind You are to me, and how little I have deserved Your kindness!

13. In Your strength I shall have power over the enemies of my soul. Neither poisoned words nor great strength shall be able to harm me.

14. You will say to my soul: "Put your trust in Me and I will deliver you; you shall have My sure protection. You shall know My name, that you may call Me at once to your assistance."

15. Help me, then, O Lord, for I will cry to You and trust that You will hear me. Be with me when I am in trouble; snatch me from danger, and give me the glory of serving You faithfully.

16. As a last blessing, show me yet more of Your Son, my salvation. Grant me time to contemplate Your goodness and kindness to me during my whole life.

INTROIT

This begins with verses 15 and 16, and its psalm verse is 1. Time to contemplate God's goodness is the present time of Lent, as St. Paul writes in his letter to the Corinthians: "Here is the time of pardon; the day of salvation...we must do everything to make ourselves acceptable." The whole motive of Lent is *the need of doing penance, the value of working for salvation.* The Church never says that mortification is beautiful in itself; but she does say that when it reveals our desire to become more Christ-like, it is a manifestation of our love. That "love motive" will make even the slightest act very valuable. So, in love, we will cry (*invocabit*) and our cry will reach up to catch God's ear.

The music of *exaudiam* shows our effort to turn our own ears towards God, to catch the message He has for us. Notice the sweetness of *eum* in the four places where it occurs: the first and second are echoed in the third and fourth—our turning to Him. Again the theme of our New Year resolution (to seek the glory of God in the will of God) is amplified for us in the music of *glorificabo*. All our Lenten plans must have that one motive: His glory. See the visual translation of "length of days" in *longitudine*, as if we sing: "No matter how many days, if only they stretch out one after the other, I can use them to promote His glory through my own love for Him by developing that love in the hearts of others." Compare the music of today's Introit with that of Trinity Sunday. See how the words of the latter are like a grand summing up of Lent.

GRADUAL — Psalm 90:11-12.

This and the Tract are almost too long to allow any minute consideration of all this beautiful music. In the Gradual, verses 11 and 12 are sung. The melody is one that is very familiar, and should be easy to sing.

TRACT — Psalm 90:1-7;11-16.

This includes nearly all of Psalm 90; only verses 8, 9, and 10 are omitted. Outstanding (at a glance) are some passages. *Qui habitat*: this makes us think how firmly and solidly established are those who dwell with God. Other thought-provoking pictures may be found in the music of the following: *Dei caeli*; *Dicet Domino*; *Deus meus*; *sperabo in eum*; *sperabis*; *In manubus portabunt te*; *glorificabo eum*; *salutare meum*.

OFFERTORY

Here verse 4 and the first sentence of verse 5 are used: "As I offer myself and all I am and all I have with Thee, O Lord, I need have no fear that I am losing anything or that I shall be in the way of danger, for the shadow of Your broad shoulders (strength) will keep me hidden as a chick is beneath the wings of the mothering hen. Your truth will be my shield of right principles."

In the music of *Scapulis suis obumbrabit* we can almost see the wide shoulders that denote the strength which is to be our strength. See how *tibi* scales the heights, and how sweet is the Name of *Dominus*; the canopy provided by *et sub pennis ejus*, and how our hope (*sperabis*) reaches unto God. The strength of our shield (*scuto*) cannot be pierced as long as God is round about us, as in *circumdabit*; for His truth (*veritas ejus*) is that of heaven.

COMMUNION – Psalm 90:4-5.

In this the same words are sung, but to a different musical setting. However, the music presents the same picture as the one in the Offertory. The only exception to be noted is in the music of the last two words, *veritas ejus*. There is a sweet complacency about that music, which seems to say: "I was right! If I give myself up to You, trust in You, rely on Your promises, every good gift will be mine. Oh, how sweet is this truth!"

Psalm 90 can be a beautiful meditation for us all during Lent. During this holy season we shall be tempted in those things in which we are notably weak. It would be a great victory for the evil one if he could make us proud of our penances and prayers during these forty days; if he could induce us to be less tolerant of others who are not keeping Lent as we do; if our temper would become a scourge to all around us! These wrong attitudes may result, unless we realize that from the start we could not be able to do even one of our works of penance, were it not for the confidence that God gives us of working through Him and with Him. We can fail if we neglect to make our Lenten life a matter of love.

SECOND SUNDAY OF LENT

In the early Church there was no special Mass for today. The ceremonies of Ember Saturday were of such length that the Mass carried over to Sunday morning. That is why the Gospel of today's Mass is the same as yesterday's. The Introit and other sung parts of today's Mass were borrowed from other sources and adapted to today's Mass. There is a brightness about this day's liturgy, not only from the reflection of the Lord's transfiguration, but more especially from the words of St. Paul's Epistle: "This is the will of God: your sanctification"; and the Gospel gives us a glimpse of what awaits those who do the will of God.

INTROIT – Psalm 24:6,3,22,1-2.

"O Lord, let me not forget the mercy You showed to me in the past, and all Your kindnesses. My enemies shall not triumph over me, for I hope in You, O God, to deliver me from all that would keep me from one day seeing Your glory.—To You, O Lord, I lift up my soul; I beg You to give me this grace: that I may be able at all times to lift up my soul to You. You alone can save me from the shame of forgetting You."

The music of the Introit is restrained, no note reaching above the third line. It is like a musing reverie. I recall *miserationum tuarum* because—and note the emphasis—they are God's, not mine. The same is true of *misericordiae tuae*. Hear the determination of *ne unquam*. Then the meditation turns to vocal prayer: *libera nos*, free us, with the accent on "us." Note the simple faith in *Deus* and the sweetness of *Israel*. Free us *ex omnibus*, from all things of this earth that cause us anguish (*angustiis nostris*).

In the Collect we admit our lack of virtue and beg God to keep our body and soul directed toward Him, according to St. Paul's advice to the Thessalonians: "We gave you a pattern of how you ought to live so as to please God, and you are living by it; make more of it than ever." See how aptly the Gradual and the Tract follow with a prayer of petition, humility, and thanksgiving.

GRADUAL – Psalm 24:17-18.

"Free me, O Lord, from all trouble of mind and from all anxiety about the future. I will not try to hide my lowliness from You, or the trouble that I have to keep in the right way; but I will ask You, my kind Lord, to forgive me all my sins." The *tribulationes* seem to be great, but notice that the emphasis of the music is on *mei*. How true it is that we bring tribulations on ourselves by not keeping "in the way" of God. So, too, we dilate (*dilatatae sunt*) those tribulations by letting them "get us down."

At *de necessitatibus*, again the accent is on *meis*; the *eripe* reaches up to heaven because it is more a prayer for firmness than one seeking relief; and the *Domine* is full of loving confidence that our prayer will be granted. I always thought that the next verse was like a jolly priest friend, who used to say that he was the little violet of all humility and very proud of it! *Vide humilitatem meam et laborem meum* really means: "You can see how lacking I still am in humility and how much of self there is in my labors—all my *laborem* reaching very far, up and down.

And so, dear Lord, dismiss from them all my sinfulness." Once again the accent of the music is on *mea* in *peccata mea*.

TRACT – Psalm 105:1-4.

"I thank You, O Lord, for Your goodness, for Your everlasting mercy. Who is able to tell of all Your wondrous works? Who is able to set down all that demands our praise of You? Bless me, O Lord, that I may be just in all my dealings with others. Keep me in mind; I am one of Your own people. Come to me and lead me safely along the way to You."

In the new Psalter, *Confitemini* is changed to *Agimus Domino* (Let us give ourselves to the Lord). In that light we can understand the music of the first word—a giving of self. *Domino* is very reverent, and *bonus* is like all good, far-reaching. *Loquetur* is like a fine sermon leading souls to *Domini*. How blessed are the *beati* who attend to His judgment and imitate His justice, which is of heaven. *Memento* is like a passionate knocking on the gates of heaven. May God hear us lovingly as our song importunes Him, and may His salvation visit all the peoples of the earth!

OFFERTORY – Psalm 118:47-48.

"The thought that I am doing Your will shall be my comfort, O God. Your will is my delight. I will lift up my hands to You, my good God, and will take my delight in serving You. By the help of Your grace, I shall grow strong in the perfection to which You have invited me."

There is the true nature of prayer in the music of *Meditabor*: lifting our hearts to God, because His *mandatis* are heavenly commands. Simple music, but apt, is in *dilexi valde*. See in *levabo manus meas* the offering of the host on the paten. We are transported by that offering to a delight (*dilexi*) which is much fuller than the previous one, because our offering is now united to the one made by Him to the eternal Father in our name. Now it can be very profitable to us, as the Secret prayer indicates.

COMMUNION – Psalm 5:2-4.

Our Lord, transfigured, has come into our souls to transfigure us. It is good for us to be here, so we cry out: "Hear my prayer, O Lord, and listen to me. I want to be Your most faith-

ful subject, my King and my God, so I come to You in prayer
the first thing in the morning, before I engage in any other work.
I want to give you the first fruits of the day, the first place in my
thoughts!"

The first three notes strain to reach up to Him, transfigured
before us, as our prayer (*orationis*) rises up to Him. *Rex* and *Deus*
are very simple: we feel that we don't need to add anything to
the faith that makes us express His dominion over us. *Orabo*
again reaches up to Tabor, and there is a quiet, peaceful holiness
in *Domine*. May the vision our eyes have seen, our souls tasted,
and our song expressed so briefly, be but the foretoken of the
same thing for eternity.

THIRD SUNDAY OF LENT

All of today's liturgy would make a splendid examen for
seminarians on their observance of the seminary Rule. Lent is a
good time to set aside a whole Sunday for this purpose, and this
particular Sunday seems especially suited to such a study. Our
fastings, our self-denials can become pleasing to us after a little
while, and we may begin to judge our observance of Lent thereby.
How many chances for real self-denial, though, do we look for
in a strict observance of the Rule? The poor Rule—what violence
it suffers! And yet a spiritual writer maintains that there is an
empty niche in every religious house, awaiting the statue of the
first member of that house who keeps the Rule in its entirety!
Faithful observance can make saints or sinners, for God and the
Rule are one; the Rule is the voice of God, interpreted by our
superiors. The force of this truth is in the words of the Introit.

INTROIT – Psalm 24:15-16, 1-2.

"My eyes shall look up to You, Lord, and hope in You. I'll
not turn to myself and my own troubles, because You will release my feet from all that impedes them. Look kindly upon me,
Lord, and let me know mercy, for without You I am alone and
do very poorly." The psalm verse is a repetition of last Sunday:
"To You, O Lord, I lift up my soul; I beg You to give me this
grace: that I may be able at all times to lift up my soul to You.
You alone can save me from the shame of forgetting You."

See the eyes raised to God at *Oculi mei,* and hear the vehement protestation of *semper.* At the sweetness of the Lord's Name (*Dominum*) we drop the "eyes of our voice," realizing that we have not always used our eyes in heaven with Him. Recalling that all help to our stumbling feet comes from God, we rise again (*de laqueo pedes meos*). Consider the music of *respice in me*: God in heaven is looking—where? Down on me! And just as our voices begin to plead for mercy, each of us can recall that the reason we need mercy is not because of God, but because of *mei.* What a "come down"! This thought is paralleled again at *unicus* and *pauper sum ego.* The psalm tone lifts each soul (*animam meam*) beautifully back to the Triune God, to whom may glory be given, as it is now given, and always shall be!

St. Paul's Epistle concludes with the words: "Live as those who are native to the light. Where the light has its effect, all is goodness and holiness and truth." This admonition is followed by a timely prayer, the Gradual.

GRADUAL — Psalm 9:20,4.

"Arise, O Lord; let not human nature prevail in us, but make us subject to Your law and to Your kind providence at all times. The enemy who tempts us and tries to rob our souls of joy shall be driven away and shall perish before Your face, O God, our Protector."

The music at *Exsurge* is symbolic of the Sun of Justice rising at our prayer, to enlighten the darkness of our souls. That light, of course, comes from the Lord; and so *Domine* not only portrays the effect in the arrangement of the notes, but also in its clear, beautiful melody. *Non praevaleat* is a fervent cry; and *homo* gives us a picture of a man reaching into heaven to work his evil designs against souls. The *judicentur gentes* continues the cry, *praevaleat*; but *gentes* ends the same as *Domine* above, as if the cry for judgment ties up with that of *Domine.* The phrase *in conspectu tuo* (in Thy sight) is very beautiful. Notice the similarity of this phrase and that of *facie tua,* which follows.

TRACT — Psalm 122:1-3.

This Tract, one can note at a glance, has little variation in the music. That is because the theme is one: "In the religious life,

I find I have to keep my eyes constantly fixed on You, my God, who art in heaven, and plead with You to have mercy on me for my daily negligences. As a careless servant can learn to be perfect in service by constant attention to his master, or as a maidservant can learn by keeping her eyes on the hands of her mistress, so can I overcome my natural carelessness by keeping my eyes fixed on You, my Master. Look with pity on me—one glance of pity!"

Although one writer declares that the music of Tracts is seldom expressive of the words being sung, I feel that most of the music of the liturgy conforms to the words. The *Ad te levavi* (To You have I lifted) is clearly expressive, as also are the notes on *oculos*. See, too, those who dwell in heaven, *in caelis*; the latter is expressive not only in the mere position of the notes, but also in the sweet music of the word *caelis*. There is a true parallel between that and the passage *Ecce sicut*...; and the music is practically the same for both.

In the next verse, note the similarity between *oculi nostri* and the *oculos meos* above; they express one and the same idea. The last verse begins with the same strain as *Ecce sicut* and *Et sicut*, but the development is different; we realize that we have not been faithful servants or watchful handmaids, and so our cry is for pity (*miserere nobis*). The *Domine* certainly sings of the God of mercy; and the last two words end on a plea, which is full of the confidence filling a soul that knows God's mercy will be given to those who continually recall their own shortcomings and seek His help. This, at least, is one Tract that belies the statement, "Tracts seldom touch the domain of expressive music."

OFFERTORY – Psalm 18:9-12.

"Keep me close to Your justice, as it has been made known to me, O Lord, and make my joy consist in being faithful to my Rule, esteeming it more than any delight of lift. Let my only reward be that I keep Your Rule most exactly."

This simple prayer is as simply sung. There is great serenity about all the music of this Offertory, denoting prayerfulness and confidence. Just as our own offertory is something personal, so the words and music of today's liturgy seem to say, "This is just between God and me." The music of *Domini* is repeated on *rec-*

tae, corda, and *dulciora.* The music of *mel et favum* is as sweet as it should be; and the serious emphasis of *custodiet ea* is very properly driving the point home to us.

COMMUNION – Psalm 83:4-5.

"The sparrow finds a home for herself, and the dove a nest in which to lay her young. My home and my nest are in the choir where I may be with You, my King and my God. Happy are they who, in this life, find a home in the same place where You dwell, and where they may begin even here the work of praise that is to occupy them throughout eternity."

Look back to the music of today's Introit and see the similarity. That one thought, of keeping our eyes lifted to God, runs through the whole Mass and Office. We have just received Him who had not whereon to lay His head. He has found a place now in our hearts. How aptly our song should be from Psalm 83! Surely the aforementioned critic of the Tract would be able to see the word-painting in the first words of this Communion. One can almost see the sparrows hopping about over these words, their little wings flapping up and down.

At *altaria* the music becomes more serious. Note the strength of *virtutum,* and the condescension of *Rex meus et Deus meus.* The happiness of *beati* is restrained, except for the thought of dwelling on high with God in *domo tua*—because His house here on earth should ever be a figure of that eternal home where we hope to dwell. The last phrase, *in saeculum saeculi laudabunt te,* begins hopefully and ends very prayerfully. All in all, this is a joyful thanksgiving after holy Communion, as if the communicant should say: "The birds of the air have nests that perish, but I have been brought into Your house, O Lord, fed with Your own Body and Blood, and been given the promise of eternally abiding with You. Thanks, dear Lord! Let me prove my gratitude today and always by a stricter observance of Your law, my Rule, only for the purpose of imitating You more perfectly, only to prove my loving obedience to Your word."

LAETARE (FOURTH) SUNDAY

Like any good mother, the Church is always mindful of her children. Perhaps, after three weeks, our fasts and penances are beginning to sadden us. Our Mother the Church does not want that to happen, so she tells us of the good Bread that will be our food to reward our efforts. "Remember," she seems to say, "you are not alone in your work of sacrifice; the whole Mystical Body is one with you. There is no cause for sorrow; only joy should fill your hearts because you are so favored. How much greater would be the self-denial of others who have not had your privilege of living God's life; with what joy would they go to even greater degrees of mortification! Your acts of self-denial may lead souls to God. Therefore your sacrifices should increase with each day's new opportunities."

INTROIT – Isaias 66:10-11; Psalm 121:1.

Abbot Smith takes the word "Jerusalem" to mean community life: "Rejoice, Jerusalem, and come together, all you that love the holy city of God; rejoice happily, all you who have tasted of sorrow; for now you may taste of the consolations with which God shall be made pleasing to you.—As soon as I learn to trust You, my God, the community life becomes a joy, for I recognize the goodness of those who live with me, and we go together into Your house. May unending songs of gratitude arise to You, O Triune God!"

There is quiet joy in the music of *Laetare*, and the five notes on *Jerusalem* seem to be the steps by which we go up to the holy city. Then *conventum facite* (gather togather), with a repetition of the music of *-ventum* at *faci*, gives a picture of people gathering together; and the music on *te* seems to show a settling down. Of high station and low, *omnes qui diligitis eam* are indicated by very tender music; and the next phrase is full of restrained joy. Hear the consideration that is shown for those *qui in tristitia fuistis*; but how quickly the music rises in the next two phrases of joy. The final phrase, *consolationis vestrae*, has all the tenderness of *qui diligitis* above. The music of the psalm verse is very simple, but it has a firmness in it that bespeaks the determination of those who go into God's house.

49

GRADUAL – Psalm 121:1,7.

"As soon as I learn to trust You, my God, community life becomes a joy.... Give me peace, which comes from the abundance of Your grace, and the strength that will follow my corresponding with that grace."

Note the picture of the procession in *ibimus*, and *pax*, that true, lasting peace which is to be found only in heaven. When we yearn for peace, we are really hoping that heaven will begin here on earth. Note, also, the great strength of *virtute*, and the generous outpouring of *abundantia*, which is intended for us earthlings as it comes from God in *tuis*.

TRACT – Psalm 124:1-2.

There is great assurance, founded on deep faith, in the music for these words: "May my soul ever trust in You, O my Lord, with even a greater confidence than Your chosen people had when they trusted in Mount Sion. You are my holy city. You shall not be moved forever, nor shall my soul cease to dwell in You as long as I place my confidence in You. As mountains surround the holy city, so do You encompass my soul to protect it. I pray, Lord, that You will guard me now and forever."

Qui confidunt has a firmness that leads us *in Domino* right up to heaven. How majestic is *sicut mons Sion*! And the firmness of never being moved from our faith is beautifully expressed in the music of *non commovebitur in aeternum*. The holiness of Jerusalem is shown in *qui habitat*; and there is a fine variety of music in the first verse, all affirming confidence. In the next verse, the picture is one of the protecting mountains that surround us; the heights are reached when *Dominus* becomes our sure defense. In *populi sui* we have again a picture of God's people gathering together *ex hoc nunc*, and there is a promise of the never-endingness of eternity in *saeculum*.

OFFERTORY – Psalm 134:3,6.

"I will sing praise to You, O Lord, for Your great mercy and goodness to me. How sweet is Your holy Name to me! I will happily sing Your praises in the Divine Office, for You have made Your holy will come to pass even on earth and in heaven."

The music alone gives the picture of monks in a community quietly singing the Divine Office. The *laudate* is very prayerful, as is *Dominum*. One must note again how reverently the composer always hymns God's holy Name. Truly benign is *benignus est*, and *psallite* is like a psalm tone. The sweetness of *suavis est* is apparent, and there is a feeling of awe surrounding *omnia quaecumquae voluit*. Probably the most expressive music to be found in this Offertory is in the last five words, *in caelo et in terra*. That expressiveness is fitting, for in the Offertory we have just renounced our own wills in our personal offertory, mindful of the petition in the Lord's Prayer that God's will may be done on earth as it is in heaven. Both words and music here help us to seal that offering.

COMMUNION – Psalm 121:3-4.

"The Jerusalem of my own religious Order is a city I may be proud of, for it is part of Your own life, O Lord. It is an order that has attracted good souls from all nations to carry on Your work and to praise Your holy Name."

The music is very simple, little more than mere statement of facts. Surely each listener can picture, in the music of *Jerusalem*, his own community. Most worthy of note in all this simple music is that on *tribus, tribus Domini*: those people or tribes who have not yet heard of God, but who, through our prayers and labors may be brought to bow down to our one, true God. And once more we see the loving respect with which God's Name is regarded in *nomini tuo, Domine*. May He who is daily the joy of our souls keep us ever faithful to our vocation, strong in faith, and looking only for the day of reward promised to those who are constant in spreading His gospel, in doing His holy will.

PASSION SUNDAY

INTROIT – Psalm 42:1-2.

Up to and including the first half of the psalm verse, this Introit is typical of the day. Reading the words, let us consider them as our Lord's own, addressed to His eternal Father. "O my God, be my advocate, and show me how I can stand before You, apart from all who do iniquity, from all who have no regard for sanctity, and from all who are deceitful. You alone, my God, are the strength on which I can rely.—Send forth Your light, that I may see, and show me Your truth, that I may know Your will. By Your power and favor, I have been able to come to Your holy hill, into religion and to Your tabernacle here, where You dwell among men."

Our Lord in the Garden of Gethsemane sees all those who are about "to do iniquity" to Him: Judas, the soldiers, the chief priests, the judges, and He asks for strength to hold Himself aloof from men of their ilk. He prays for light, but none seems to come to Him in His dark hour. Yet never for a moment does He fail in His adherence to His Father's will. A second reading of the Introit makes it our own. We have to mingle with the world, with some who have no regard for sanctity; so our prayer is for strength to keep ourselves close to God at all times.

God, by His power, has called us to holy hills, to dwell close to His tabernacle. Unlike our Lord in the Garden of Gethsemane, we are never deprived of the Holy Spirit's light, or of strength from God, when we call upon Him for these aids. In the music, *Judica* is timid, as if we fear the judgment; but *Deus* brings us up close to God, and we lose our fear as we recall that His mercy is above all His works. A heavenly cause is *causam meam*; but *de gente non sancta* indicates the earth. Hear the cry in *eripe me*, the confidence in *quia tu es Deus meus*, and the strength in *fortitudo*.

GRADUAL – Psalm 142:9-10.

This is a beautiful prayer and confession: "Deliver me, O Lord, from the bitter enemies of my soul, for I have run to You for refuge. Teach me to do Your will. Rid me, O Lord, of the

evil in my own nature, the evil desires and tendencies that I have
encouraged in my past life. Rescue me from the injustice I have
practiced against You, robbing You of my heart, which was
Yours by right."

In the music, notice the difference in this *Eripe* from that of
the Introit. In the latter, it was our first cry. Since then we have
prayed in the Collect for God to look favorably down upon us;
and in the Epistle we have heard the words of St. Paul: "Shall
not the Blood of Christ, who offered Himself, through the Holy
Spirit, as a victim unblemished in God's sight, purify our con-
sciences, and set them free from lifeless observance, to serve the
living God?"

Yes, now we have confidence, so we linger lovingly on the
Eripe, and the *Domine* is a grateful prayer. See the number of
our enemies in *inimicis meis*, and the wide variety of things contained in *voluntatem tuam*. Because we are happy that God is to
free us, our voices rise to great heights on *Liberator meus*, and
again our thanks for this liberation is spoken in *Domine*. In *a
viro* we see men who belong to God as we do, but in *iniquo* we
see the terrible depths to which even those once in God's friendship may fall. No wonder we hasten to cry again for help—*eripies
me!*

TRACT – Psalm 128:1-4.

This is a splendid prayer of faith and confidence and trust
in God: "My soul has gone through many temptations from the
time of my youth upwards, and these have been serious trials,
often leading me to lose heart. But now I know that You, O
Lord, allowed these temptations to assail me, many of which I
have with Your help been able to overcome, that I may know
Your kind care of me and put my trust in You. Evil spirits have
caused me to suffer much and have made my life a burden. They
have prolonged their torments upon me. But I trust in Your
justice, O Lord; You will put aside all those who hinder me in
my path to You."

The music of *Saepe* indicates graphically the many rises and
falls of grace *a juventute mea* (from the time of my youth) in both
instances. The music of *Etenim* has the meaning of "however"
and the joy that is in the soul of one who realizes whence comes

strength for the fight. In *supra...peccatores* one can almost see
the enemies surrounding a person—about his shoulders, on his
back, at every side—prolonging their iniquities. The force of
Etenim is enough to assure us that God will hew down those
enemies of our souls—see Him cutting them down on the last
three phrases of *torum*—if we continue faithfully with the perse-
vering thought of *Etenim*.

OFFERTORY – Psalm 118:17,107.

In the Gospel, our Lord tells the Jews that one reason for
their perseverance in evil is the fact that they are "not of God."
In this Offertory, we give Him assurance that, by offering our
hearts and our wills to Him, we try to be "of God." Each one
declares: "My praise of You, O Lord, shall be in the uprightness
and sincerity of my heart, for my true life comes from You. I
beseech You to give me a full life, that I may keep all Your
commands. Quicken me, O Lord, according to Your promise."

Confitebor finds us scaling the heights in music that is not
unfamiliar. This introduction is used frequently, but always in
passages that lift us up to heaven. (See also: *Rorate*, Introit of
First Sunday of Advent; the antiphons of the first and third
psalms of the Vespers of that same Sunday; the Invitatory of
Christmas; the Introit of St. Thomas, December 29; the Offertory
for the Feast of the Holy Name of Jesus, almost a repetition;
also the Magnificat antiphon for second Vespers of the same
feast; the first antiphon for first Vespers of the Feast of the Holy
Family; the Offertory of the second Sunday after Epiphany; the
Magnificat antiphon for the sixth Sunday after Epiphany, and
the Magnificat antiphon of last Sunday. We shall find many more
instances of this same music as we go on through the year.) See
the fullness of *in toto corde meo*. At *retribue* there is the feeling of
"Turn Your eyes down on Your servant, O Lord." And as result, we find firmness in the promise to watch over words and
actions (*et custodiam sermones tuos*). Hear the heavenly message
in *verbum*, and the adoration and love in pronouncing the Lord's
Name (*Domine*).

COMMUNION – 1 Corinthians 11:24-25.

St. Thomas Aquinas says, in the antiphon *O Sacrum Con-
vivium*, that the holy Eucharist is a sacrament in which the mem-

ory of Christ's passion is renewed. How apt it is that on Passion Sunday, after having had our souls nourished by the Food of angels, we sing: "This is My Body, which is to be given up for you; this cup is the new testament in My Blood. ...Do this, whenever you consume it, for a commemoration of Me."

How simply we sing these first words, in awe and reverence, as our Lord must have said them on the first Holy Thursday. The only place we ascend to any great heights in the music is at *hoc facite quotiescumque sumitis*, as if He says to us: "Oh, remember, whenever you partake of this sacred Banquet, at what a terrible price it was prepared for you. Remember the love that inspired that gift. Remember of what and of whom it is a commemoration." This is a fitting close to the Mass of Passion Sunday. May our love throughout Passiontide be ever ready to reach such great heights because of the incomparable love-gift that is daily ours.

PALM SUNDAY

The music of both the blessing of the palms and the procession will not be gone into at length, but one cannot help but note how much like the chants at Mass the first part of the blessing is. *Hosanna filio David* is like an Introit. The other parts, the procession hymns, the *Gloria laus* and the *Ingrediente* are all word pictures of unforgettable melodies. In the last named, see the entry at *Ingrediente*. See the children climbing into the trees to get branches at *Hebraeorum pueri*; and see the waving of branches, from *Cum ramis* to the end. But when we come to the Introit of the Mass, the scene changes.

INTROIT — Psalm 21:20,22,2.

Here we find a current of sadness in both the words and the music. "O Lord, do not go far from me; in Your mercy, be my defense and save me; save me, humbled by the thought of my sins, from the evil spirits and all their fury. My God, my God, why have You forsaken me? Look upon me. This is Your cry, O Lord, on the Cross; and it is also my cry, for it seems to me, at times, that You have really forsaken me. What You could not

say upon the Cross, Lord, I can truly say: that my sins stand in
the way of my profiting wholly by the salvation that You have
won for me."

The near repetition of the music on *Domine* and again at *ne
longe facias* shows the depths that our hearts have reached. As we
think of the help He is always ready to give us, if we will but
make an effort to lift ourselves up from the earth, we begin to
rise (*auxilium tuum* and *defensionem meam*). Then hear the heart-
rending cry in *aspice*: "Look, O Lord, and see how much need
I have of Your defending me!" From there on, the music of the
Introit seems to take a more confident note. "I have called for
God to look after me, and I know He will free me from those
enemies of my soul who are as ferocious as the lion and the uni-
corn. Because I do not trust in myself but trust in Him, because
of this humility on my part, He will save me."

GRADUAL – Psalm 72:24,1-3.

This has been beautifully paraphrased by Abbot Smith: "In
Your kindness, O Lord, You have let me see Your constant care
for me; and Your divine will, I now see, has led me and guided
me. You have offered me such glory with You that all the goods
of earth are as nothing. Oh, how good You are, dear God, to
them that seek You, to them that are upright in heart. How good
You are to them who walk before You, striving with their whole
hearts after the perfection to which You have called them. A
temptation arose in my mind, and it almost caused me to slip
and stumble, for I saw the prosperity of the wicked, and I was
almost tempted to envy them."

Perhaps, apart from monasteries given to chanting the entire Mass and Office, in only a few places will today's Gradual
and Tract be sung in their entirety. This is because of their length
and that of today's Gospel (Passion). But even though we may
not sing it, just a glance at the music will be interesting. Do you
remember how as children we would walk along with a big
brother or sister and he or she would hold us by the hand? In
Tenuisti manum dexteram meam see God walking along with your
right hand in His, swinging hands happily in the protection that
is yours. In *Deduxisti me*, each knows that if we have ever been
led to great heights, it has always been because God was leading

us. There is deep, grateful affection in *Quam bonus Deus* and a great lifting up to those who are right of heart (having pure intention) in *rectis corde*. And so, through the remainder of the Gradual the words are graphically pictured by the music.

TRACT — Psalm 21:2-9,18-19,22,24,32.

" 'My God, my God, why have You forsaken me? Look upon me.' This was Your cry, O Lord, on the Cross; and it is also my cry, for it seems to me at times that You have really forsaken me. What You could not say upon the Cross, Lord, I can truly say: that my sins stand in the way of my profiting wholly by the salvation You have won for me. I cry to You in the light, and it seems to me that You do not hear. I cry to You in the waking moments of the night; let not my voice sound to You as a fool's cry that comes not from the heart! But I can find You in the holy place of the choir, where the praises of Your servants are sung.

"There the voices of Your saints, who have led or are leading holy lives, mingle with my sinful voice. They cried to You, and they were made safe; their hope in You was not in vain. Hear me now, Lord; let my cry be heard and my hope be strengthened as was that of Your saints. I am a worm, fit only to live in the earth; and by my inclinations to evil I am scarcely human! I am a fit object of scorn, and worth only to be driven out from among Your people. If Your people knew me as You, my good God, know me, they would surely scoff at me! They would speak hard things against me, and shake their heads at me as if I were of no account; and, dear Lord, they would have ample cause. If people scorned and reviled You on the Cross, You who were infinitely innocent, what scorn would my contemporaries not justly heap on me?

"They cried out at You, my Lord, reproaching You because You were in their power; and Your Father allowed You to be scorned for my sins. While I was tried, I could get no help from those who stood by me. They seemed only to think of what use they could make of me. They nailed You to the Cross, dear Lord; and You wish that I, in my small way, should suffer with You. Save me, Lord, humbled by the thought of my sins, from the beasts, the devils, and from all their fury. This shall be my testimony, to fear You and praise You, Lord. I will praise You with all reverence. Let all the children of Your saints show forth Your glory in their lives. I will, with Your grace, pass on to others Your goodness, O my God, and with Your saints I will try to increase the perfection of life to which You have called me, so that the good seed of religious life may grow up for Your glory after I shall have gone with those who shall be Your children."

Note the holy adoration of the music on the first word, *Deus*. Note the length of *Longe*, the cry of *clamabo*, the pleading supplication in *Libera me*. Towards the end of the Tract we seem to see light: in spite of the dangers about us, the darkness that covers our souls, we know from experience that the clouds will be borne away by the winds and that the sun will shine through. So the Christian's soul realizes that, after we have passed through the darkness of the passion and crucifixion, the brightness of Easter morning will make us forget the shadows.

The music takes on a more confident strain from *Qui timetis Dominum* to the end. There is a suppressed joy, but the joy of faith, the realization of things to be hoped for. *Laudate eum...magnificate eum.* "I will, by Your grace, tell other people about Your goodness, so that all may join me in blessing the Lord who has done such wondrous things for my soul."

OFFERTORY – Psalm 68:21-22.

"Dear God, when your divine Son was in desolation on the Cross, He cried: 'My heart has looked for reproach and misery. I looked for one who would grieve with Me, but there was no one; for one who would comfort Me, and I found him not. And they gave Me gall for My food.' Divine Son upon the Cross, support me now, O Lord, and let me not lose heart altogether."

The words of this Offertory should be consoling to us. We are offering ourselves to God. Our Lord in His passion looked for "one" who would grieve with Him, "one" who would comfort Him. In your religious community He finds many such a "one." Let us each make sure that our offering of self is so complete, so entire that it will serve to assuage His grief, that it will be a comfort to Him. In the music, *Improperium* drops to a depth that is not reached elsewhere in this Offertory. Each succeeding passage shows God's love welling up: *cor, miseriam, sustinui, contristaretur, consolantem, quaesivi.* But all His sighs reach a climax at *et non inveni.* There are two pictures in *siti*: first, the soldiers raising the spear with a vinegar-soaked sponge to the lips of our Lord; second, the interpretation of "I thirst for souls." May our own individual offertory of self be thirst-quenching solace and comfort to Him in His passion. And—oh, mystery of love!—the solace and comfort will come back to us in even greater measure.

COMMUNION – Matthew 26:42.

"My Father, if this chalice may not pass Me by, but I must drink it, then Your will be done." Simple words, in the simplest musical setting imaginable. But the simplest melodies are very often the most difficult to write. It could not have been simple for our Lord to say those words. Of ourselves we could not even say them, as simple as they are. But with Christ resting in our hearts, we can make those words our own, in His spirit, not only today, but especially on all those days when the Cross seems nearer and heavier. "I have given you an example," He said. Yea, more: He has just given us Himself! May we ever have the grace to say, *"Fiat voluntas tua!"* May we be so happy in doing His will that we can even sing it, in the simple but effective music applied to those words today.

HOLY THURSDAY

The Introit sung in the Mass this day is the same as that of Tuesday in Holy Week. This Introit and Wednesday's speak of the Cross, but they also bring out the glory of Him who was crucified for love of us. There is a fine picture given to us here of our Lord before He endures His awful passion, including the sacrilegious acts of the soldiers at the scourging and crowning.

INTROIT – Galatians 6:14; Psalm 66:2.

"God forbid that I should make a display of anything except the grace of our Lord Jesus Christ, in whom is our safety, our life, and our own resurrection; by Him we have been saved and liberated from eternal death.—Have mercy on me, O God, and bless me; shed the light of Your own face upon me, and have mercy on me."

These words are a glorious tribute, but the music is far from being a hymn of glory. The composer, evidently after meditating on the words, seems to realize how vain this sacrifice would be for many souls, and so his song is cast in a somewhat sad strain. How can we say that many would not share in the redemption of the Cross? The answer lies in the manner in which any crucifix is regarded outside the Church today: to some non-Catholics it is superstitious, idolatrous, because men will not admit that their sins have fashioned the Cross.

Nos autem: we, however, are we bearing our own crosses in His spirit? Do not our actions often belie our words? The words and music of this sacred day should make us realize more and more the privilege we have of sharing in the Cross through the holy Eucharist—*memoria passionis ejus*. Recall these thoughts at the *Nos autem*; then see how humble is *gloriari oportet* as a realization. All the glory is in *cruce Domini nostri Jesu Christi*! Hear the promise in *salus* and *vita*, and then see how we may arise in *resurrectio nostra* when we have been freed (*liberati sumus*).

GRADUAL – Philippians 2:8-9.

"Christ accepted an obedience that brought Him to His death on the Cross. That is why God has raised Him to such a height, and given Him that Name that is greater than any other name."

The first part of this beautiful Gradual tells us what Christ did for us; the second part tells what God did for our Lord because of His example to us. There is simplicity in the first four words; but on *nobis* the music shows us to what depths He went to do those things. The outstanding act of our Lord's life is indicated in *obediens*: His obedience, at all costs, to the will of His eternal Father, even though that obedience brought Him to death, the death of the Cross. *Propter quod* is recitative, as if to say: "But now here's the other side of the picture: because Christ descended so low for our sakes, God lifted Him to the greatest heights!" Note that rise in *illum* and the devotion in the music again on *nomen*. The recitative again at *quod est super* emphasizes the beauty and power and blessedness of that Name that is above all names.

OFFERTORY — Psalm 117:16-17.

This Offertory is the same as the one sung on third Sunday after Epiphany, and it is equally applicable here. Moreover, we may add one thought: *non moriar* seems to promise us, "He that eateth My flesh, which I leave for you today, will not die but will have life everlasting!" May our offertory and our share in the divine harvest at holy Communion help us to attain a life of eternal blessedness!

COMMUNION — John 13:12,13,15.

"Then, when the Lord Jesus had finished washing their feet and put on His garments, He sat down again, and He said to them, 'Do You understand what it is I, your Master and Lord, have done to you? I have been setting you an example that will teach you, in your turn, to do what I have done for you!"

The music of this Communion sounds like a child telling of something that has happened. Note the almost singsong sameness of the music at *postquam* and *cum* and again at *lavit*, as if the singer is going on breathlessly to tell what occurred. When it comes to the words of our Lord at *Scitis*, the narrator, perhaps unintentionally, seems to adopt the tone of Christ. Note how majestically it rises above the introductory music. Note also what seems to sound like a question mark in the music of *Dominus* and *Magister*.

The final part of this beautiful composition is as gentle as are the words, but there is a convincing strength in *vos ita faciatis*, as though our Master would say to us: "Now strengthened with this new Food from heaven, do not be afraid ever to follow My example. Be servants to all men; humble yourselves; let the love that I have given you in this sacrament of Love so fill your lives that you will gladly give yourselves to such an extent that all men one day, through you, may know of the great love I have for all the souls in the world." So be it!

INTROIT — Psalm 138:18,5-6,1-2.

Abbot Smith's paraphrase is not a literal translation by any means, but it is very beautiful and applicable for today's feast: "You have overcome death, O Lord, and are still with me; You have laid Your kind hand upon me. Your knowledge of me I cannot fathom, for the depth and the height of it are far beyond me.—You have tried me, O Lord, and You know me most intimately. You alone thoroughly understand me, far better than I have known myself."

The music of the Introit tells us immediately the nature of the feast we are celebrating. *Resurrexi* is very calm, very quiet music, as quiet as was the resurrection itself. Our Lord is speaking to His heavenly Father, so there is no glorying in it—just a quiet statement of fact, stressing the obedience of the Son to the eternal Father. It is our Lord's first prayer after rising from the dead, and there is a fervor in the music, bespeaking a great love. Dom Johner says of this: "It is all inner fervor, this melody, breathing intense love, like a song coming from the quiet, unalterable depths of eternity itself. Exclusively personal, it has no thought of its listeners; no impetuous cries of triumph disturb it...it is a smile of purest joy. It clothes the text with lights and colors to which we should otherwise have remained entirely oblivious, and thus it opens up new avenues to the understanding of the Paschal Mystery."[1]

GRADUAL — Psalm 117:24,1.

The paraphrase here is very fine: "Each day of my life is given to me by You, O God, that I may glorify You and joyfully occupy myself in Your service. My principal work is to praise You, my God, for all Your goodness, and especially for Your great and constant mercy to me."

The real joy of this feast comes in this Gradual, when the soul cannot be restrained from singing of the glorious day that has dawned. Two days ago, Good Friday, there was a dark day; but the clouds have passed, and today the Sun of Justice, in all His glory, shines through. How gently the music begins on *Haec*

[1] *op. cit.*, p. 178.

dies, and then on *quam fecit* builds up to great joy! *Dominus* sings with sheer happiness, and so do *exultemus* and *laetemur*. *Confitemini* is but a simple statement, but the music of the next three words reaches up to heaven in its beauty. Hear the reverence of *Dominus*; note the emphasis on *bonus* and to what great extent *saeculum* goes.

ALLELUIA — 1 Corinthians 5:7.

The words of this verse are from the Epistle that had just been read: "Alleluia, Christ our paschal Victim has been sacrificed for us." What joy must have filled the hearts of the new Christians of the early Church when they first heard these words, when they realized fully what it meant to have Christ as their paschal Victim, immolated for their sakes!

The music of this Alleluia is not new to us; we have had the same strain, at least parts of it, on other feasts. In *pascha nostrum* the music is elevating, as if to assure us "our pasch is not of this earth, it is something heavenly." One may wonder how such excessive heights of joy could be reached as they are on *immolatus*. It is the realization of the soul that sings, "Now that Christ has been immolated in our stead, we may cast off the burden of our sins, and through His redeeming sacrifice rise to new heights of grace." The word *Christus* is sung lovingly and gratefully.

SEQUENCE

Let all Christians offer the sacrifice of praise to the paschal Victim.

The Lamb has redeemed the sheep; Christ, the sinless One, has reconciled sinners to His Father.

Death and life contend in a wondrous encounter: the Prince of Life died, indeed; but now living, He reigns.

Tell us, Mary, what did you see in the way?

"I saw the sepulcher of the living Christ, and I saw the glory of Him that had risen; the angelic witnesses, the napkin and the linen cloths. Christ, my hope, has risen. He shall go before you into Galilee."

We know in truth that Christ has risen from the dead. O victorious King, have mercy on us!

The music of the Sequence is so simple and so beautiful that one wonders why everyone doesn't sing it. And like all true simplicity, it is very beautiful. The first exultation is at *Agnus redemit oves*; this is repeated at *Mors et vita duello* and again at *Scimus Christum surrexisse*, as if to verify the thought on *immolatus*. The last word, *miserere*, is a very humble prayer. There are other beauties hidden in the words and music of this Sequence; you will find many of them for yourselves as you study it in preparation for Easter morning.

OFFERTORY – Psalm 75:9-10.

"At some time of life, the earth stands still to let every soul know of God's will, when You, O God, come in judgment."

The music of the first part is symbolic of the words. *Terra* is the the earth; *tremuit* is like the upward sloping lines that crack the earth's surface. All is very quiet, as is *quievit*; but note the rising at *resurgeret* and again at *judicio*. *Deus* is full of awe and majesty. What a magnificent spur this Offertory should be to our offering of our own hearts and wills! In the face of the truth herein expressed, who could hold back the tiniest part of his love?

COMMUNION – 1 Corinthians 5:7-8.

"Has not Christ been sacrificed for us, our paschal Victim? Let us keep the feast, then, not with the leaven of yesterday, but with the unleavened bread, with purity, and honesty of intent."

This repeats the thought of the Epistle and the Alleluia verse; but this music is a quiet, graceful Communion song, differing greatly from the music of the Alleluia. The most salient phrase in this music is on *itaque*; it is beautiful and forceful. It seems to emphasize the "therefore." Since Christ our Pasch has been immolated for our sakes, *therefore* we should never approach His holy table to partake of the unleavened bread of His Body with anything but sincere, honest hearts. Imagine the early Christians approaching the altar for holy Communion, singing this magnificent song! May it ever be a reminder to us of the double gift awaiting us when we truly give ourselves in all humble gratitude for the boon of having been bought at so great a price.

LOW SUNDAY

The music for the Mass of this Sunday is, for the most part, extremely simple. It seems to fit nicely into the pattern of the events of this day as witnessed in the early Church. On the Saturday before Low Sunday, the newly baptized removed their white baptismal robes; on Low Sunday they were to receive their first holy Communion. How appropriately the liturgy speaks of the soul-nourishment that is to come to these new "babes of Christ."!

INTROIT — 1 Peter 2:2; Psalm 80:2.

"You are children newborn, and all your craving must be for the soul's pure milk.—I will rejoice before You, O my God, my only Helper. I will sing unto You, for You are my God." Here the music is a quiet preparation for the new feast of the soul.

Dom Johner's comment on this Introit is a thoughtful introduction to today's liturgy: "In order to preserve the supernatural life, we should have a spontaneous longing for the nourishment of our souls, for truth, and for the holy Eucharist. This is the wish of holy Mother Church. In ancient times she impressed this strongly upon the neophytes, who had put off their white baptismal robes yesterday. At present she sings it for new communicants. And with true maternal solicitude, she sings it for us all. She cries out to us: Preserve the spirit of children of God, remain simple, humble, and submissive to Him. Remain *rationabiles*, children of the spirit; do not become children of the flesh. Remain *sine dolo*; preserve the truth without falsity, and love without envy. And come to me and nourish yourselves upon the stores which Christ has confided to me. Then deep joy will fill your hearts; God will be your helper, and you will rejoice and exult in His sight."[1]

ALLELUIA — Matthew 28:7; John 20:26.

"In the day of My having risen from the dead, said the Lord, I will go before you into Galilee.—Eight days afterwards, when the doors were locked, Jesus came and stood in their midst. 'Peace be upon you, He said.' "

[1] *op. cit.*, pp. 188-89.

There is quite a contrast between the music of *In die* and that of *praecedem vos*; the latter seems to rise to great heights, as if intensifying the idea not only of preceding, but also of guiding from above. Such a great rise in music (almost an octave above the rest of the chant) is rarely met in other chants. It looks almost as if the melody for those two words was taken bodily from some other text and inserted here; when *in Galilaeam* returns to the original simplicity of the first words, this seems to be most evident.

The music of the second Alleluia and verse are new. I cannot recall that they are found in any other chant. Notice how the music of *Post dies...clausis* seems to be repeated in *stetit Jesus... suorum*. Then *Pax vobis* seems to tell us that our greatest peace will come from our Lord's having risen. Note the form of the resurrection in that music.

OFFERTORY – Matthew 28:2,5,6.

"An angel of the Lord, coming down from heaven, said openly to the women: He whom you have come to look for has risen, as He told you." This Offertory is taken from the Mass for Easter Monday. Here we have another picture of the angels of the Lord ascending and descending.

The music is angelic, too. Note the height of *caelo*. The melody is not a strange one; it is found on several other great feasts. The *mulieribus* is of heaven, too, because those holy women were the first to seek heaven's risen King. *Quem quaeritis* seems to have a question mark even in the music, and *surrexit* is also a picture of that word. It would be an interesting exercise for the choir to locate the other feasts on which this music is used and to compare the "music pictures" with the other texts. There is something majestic, stately, in this Offertory, reminding us that our individual offertory must be marked with such dignity.

COMMUNION – John 20:27.

"Let me have your hand; put it into My side. Cease your doubting, and believe." The music is of the same simplicity as the Introit and Gradual. We must remember that the Offertory is borrowed.

This Communion should be a delight to new communicants; our Lord takes each of them by the hand and bids them to keep their faith ever strong. When our Lord comes to us in holy Communion, He takes each of us, too, by the hand. May the privilege of being so near to Him, of sensing Him at our sides and in our hearts, help us to grow in faith and love!

GOOD SHEPHERD SUNDAY

INTROIT — Psalm 32:5,6,1.

"The earth is full of Your mercy and goodness, O Lord! You have created all things by Your word.—In my striving after perfection, I must not be downhearted but be joyful in Your service, O Lord." This is beautiful, tender music, which seems to marvel at God's great mercy.

His sheep are known to Him; His goodness, His love, and His mercy are all for them. Knowing the weakness of His sheep, He has compassion on them. As we recognize this truth, our hearts and voices do not leap up in praise, but we sing gratefully, in almost hushed tones, our humble gratitude. *Misericordia* is very simple music; the reverence is saved for *Domino*. Then *plena* expresses the fullness of God's mercy; *verbo* is simply sung; but *Dei* is reverent, culminating in joy at the *alleluia*.

ALLELUIA — Luke 24:35; John 10:14.

"The disciples knew the Lord Jesus in the breaking of bread. I am the Good Shepherd; My sheep are known to Me and know Me." There is great joy in the first *Alleluia* and in *Cognoverunt discipuli*, because like the disciples, we too shall know the Lord in the breaking of bread this morning. There is a twofold anticipation here. Note the acknowledgment of loving servitude in *Dominum* and the reverence in *Jesus*. We find a beautiful "picture" in just looking at the music of *fractione*: it is so like the action and motion in breaking a piece of bread. Then the soul sings at great length, in joy, on *panis*, as we look forward to that heavenly Bread that is soon to be "our daily bread."

The second *Alleluia* is a fine melody; although it is sung four times (also at *cognosco* and again at *cognoscunt*), it is not tiresome. It is a repeated joy that we are known to God and that He knows us. *Ego sum* seems to say: "I am your God, who came down from heaven just for you. I am the One who, if you stray from Me, will descend into the valley of death to lift you up, for I love you with a great love."

OFFERTORY – Psalm 62:2,5.

The Epistle of today's Mass closes with these words: "You had been like sheep going astray; now you have been brought back to Him, your Shepherd, who keeps watch over your souls." Since we know of God's watchfulness over us, our hearts cry out in the Offertory that we, too, will not be outdone in watching: "My God, I will watch for You, be on the alert for You in the early morning; You have granted me the privilege of offering all the work of my hands in Your name."

The repetition of *Deus* is like a confession on our part: "It is God, my God, who from heaven watches for me, who waits for some sign of my love." So we bring the offering of heart and will as tokens of our love. We can imagine one rising up early in the morning to look for God as *ad te de luce vigilo* is sung; hear again the fervor and honor of the music in *nomine tuo*; and see both hands lifted up in prayer, like the all-embracing *Dominus vobiscum* at *levabo manus Meas*. The final *alleluia* is one of gratitude that we have been given another chance to prove our love.

COMMUNION – John 10:14.

We have just had the great privilege of being present at the breaking of Bread. Our Lord is very close to us; He is in our poor hearts, and from that hidden fold He tells us: "I am the Good Shepherd; My sheep are known to Me and know Me."

Try to hear His voice singing these words to us. His first *alleluia* is a song of joy, but there is a note of sadness in it. Perhaps He sees in our hearts something that is not of His choosing. The sad note makes us look deeper, and we see the wrong thing, too. Then we try to eradicate it quickly, and just as quickly comes His second *alleluia*, one of quiet satisfaction. May the Good Shepherd of our souls ever find a welcome of love in our hearts: our acknowledgment of His knowledge of us, and ours of Him.

THIRD SUNDAY AFTER EASTER

The liturgy today seems to have been fitted not only to the mystery that we celebrate, but also to the season of the year, which must have been as beautiful in Palestine as it is here at our very doors. The resurrection of nature is an accomplished fact; the earth, God's earth, is adorned with color, beauty, and scent that have baffled artist, poet, and essayist. All is but the reflected beauty of the risen Lord, who so rejoices our hearts.

INTROIT – Psalm 65:1-2,3.

The realization of God's presence among us, as manifested by all nature, makes Abbot Smith's paraphrase very apt: "I will sing joyfully to You, O God, with all the earth. I will praise You in psalms and glorify Your holy Name.—How great are Your works, O Lord! They strike me with fear. Your strength is so great that your enemies cringe before You."

Other translations of the last four words say, "enemies lie to You"; but for those who do not understand Latin, there must be confusion as to what "lie" means. The word "cringe" is far better since it carries the idea of servile fear, deception, cowardice. It seems to ask, "Now, with all nature reflecting God's glory, who can deny that Christ, our loving Lord, is God?" The opening Latin words of the Introit are all in the imperative mood: Be joyful! Give glory! Say to the Lord! The music emphasizes the commands on *Jubilate, psalmum dicite, date gloriam.* Each is like a trumpet call, a spontaneous cry of the soul. As usual, there is very tender music on the words *nomini ejus.*

ALLELUIA – Psalm 110:9; Luke 24:46.

"I will never cease to thank You, Lord, for the redemption You have won for Your people.—It was fitting that Christ should suffer, and should rise again from the dead, and so enter into His glory." As if to make atonement for the cringers, this music gaily sings.

The first *Alleluia* is a familiar one; we sang it several times during Christmastide (third Mass on Christmas; feast of St. Stephen; feast of St. John). The music of *Redemptionem* is symbolic of the act, raising us up to heaven; of *misit*, its coming down

69

to us from heaven; of *populo suo*, wherever God's people are over the face of the earth. In the second *Alleluia* note the repetition of each of the two phrases after the asterisk; if either repetition were omitted, the music would not sound nearly so complete as it does.

The music of *Oportebat* is emphasized as if it would remind us of the necessity of our Lord's having to suffer. Some students of the liturgy believe that originally the word arrangement was *et a mortuis resurgere*, but that the more eloquent sequence of words was written by a Latin scholar. The music would seem to give force to this theory; that of *resurgere* seems as if it might have been written for *a mortuis*. The words *et ita intrare in gloriam suam* need no explanation; in the very picture that the notes make, the meaning is quite clear. What is of interest, however, is the repetition on *suam*. Time and again our Lord told us that all He did was for the glory of the Father, and He never failed to urge His listeners to do likewise.

OFFERTORY – Psalm 145:2.

"The chief work of my life is to sing Your praises, O my God! Give me such an interest in it that I shall be content to do this same work for You in all my life." The music of the first part of this Offertory fits splendidly into Abbot Smith's paraphrase. There is merely a statement of fact, in both words and music.

When the singer realizes what a privilege it is, *laudabo Dominum* reaches up to God, because that privilege is granted not only for today but for always—*in vita mea*. Some of the other verses in Psalm 145 (verses not sung today) amplify this idea: "You are my Helper; let my hope be fixed in You. You are all-powerful and can make even the praise I render to You acceptable...Oh, reign forever in my soul! You are always good to me and will be so forever, if I but stay close to You, O my God." Both words and music of this beautiful prayer should effect a calmness in us as we offer ourselves to be co-victims with the paschal Victim.

COMMUNION – John 16:16.

This is like our Lord's answer to our offering of self: "After a little while you will see Me no longer; and again after a little

while you will have sight of Me, because I go to the Father."
With the eyes of faith we see Him now through the liturgy, and
shall continue to do so until Ascension Day. Then for a little
while, until Christmas, we shall not "see" Him except through
the memory of His having been with us.

How much more favored we are than were the apostles!
They had to wait until they joined Him in heaven; but we "see"
Him daily in the white altar bread that becomes our Communion
Host. And we "see" Him in the ever-recurring liturgical seasons
and holydays. Note how matter-of-fact are *Modicum* and *non
videbitis me*; we can almost hear our Lord saying them in this
music. The promise of heaven is in *iterum*.... Since His words
were said before Good Friday, the music of *vado ad Patrem*, instead of ascending as one would expect, goes down into the grave
of death. The repeated, happy *alleluia* that follows tells of our
joy at the realization of His being once more in heaven.

There is a profound meditation in this Communion alone.
The *modicum* of life is but a little while, compared with eternity;
the *modicum* of His presence in our hearts each day is but the
praemium vitae aeternae of which St. Thomas Aquinas sang. But
both give ample promise of the *vitae aeternae* if we spend both
modicums entirely with and for Him. What a rich harvest awaits
us! See what God's love has done; see what love can do!

FOURTH SUNDAY AFTER EASTER

INTROIT – Psalm 97:1-2,1.

"O my God, I will sing a new song to You every day, because You are ever most wonderful in Your patience with me.
You have shown the beautiful life of Your Son to the whole
world.—You alone give me the victory; and when I fail, it is because I trust in myself and not in You. The victory is not for
myself but for You, because I am Yours."

When the music of this Introit is sung, it may seem strangely
familiar. Looking back we find that the Introit of Low Sunday
was similar to today's in many parts. Compare the two for yourself and note how, in both, the words and music make a unified

picture. The music does not carry a great shout for victory, but is quietly sung as a hymn of thanksgiving. The eternal Father has made known His justice to all nations; and having accepted His Son's sacrifice for our sakes, He now has glorified His Son.

See how reserved is the music of *Cantate...canticum novum*, so typical of the spirit of the chant in the Church. There is a gradual rise in the melody (if it were all written on one line straight across the page, we could draw a line that would rise steadily from the first note of the Introit to the second note on *brachium*), which reaches its height on *mirabilia*. The picture of spreading abroad God's mercy is evident on *revelavit*. This whole Introit is a lesson in Gregorian Chant: When you sing to the Lord, let your song be one of reverent joy that is restrained. Our song today cannot be a new one, but it can be one of renewed love, in the same spirit in which our Lord sang a new canticle to the glory of the Father as He rose from the dead on Easter morn. The deeper we penetrate into God's love for us, the more loving will be our renewed canticle.

ALLELUIA – Psalm 117:16; Romans 6:9.

"Take me in Your right hand, O my God, and raise my soul to You. By Your right hand I shall be saved.—Christ, now that He has risen from the dead, cannot die any more; death has no power over Him." Psalm verse 17, not used here, is replaced by the passage from St. Paul which resembles verse 17: "In Your strength, I shall be saved from death, and my soul, living with Your life, shall praise You and shall show to others the goodness You have shown me."

We are familiar with the words after the first *Alleluia*; we sang them on the third Sunday after Epiphany and again on Holy Thursday. Both former occasions were in anticipation. To-day we sing them after realizing the value of being lifted up by our risen Lord. In the first *Dextera* God's hand comes down to lift us up; and this is more evident in the second *dextera*. In *fecit virtutem* we have a picture of God's hand scattering His largess upon our souls. And *exaltavit me* portrays the heights to which His grace exalts us.

The three groups of rising notes on *Christus, resurgens,* and *ex mortuis* are vivid pictures of the resurrection and may be regarded as the three days in the grave. Then *non moritur* seems to say, "He who arose will never again descend to the tomb." The music of *mors* is as glorious as was the purpose of His death for us. Although the *non dominabitur* but follows the line of the *Alleluia*, yet it is glorious in its own right as it tells us that death has been conquered.

OFFERTORY – Psalm 65:1-2,16.

This is described in the notes for the second Sunday after Epiphany. See how truly the same idea applies to today's liturgy. Our risen Lord is the one who stands on the heights, bidding us to come and hear what marvelous things the eternal Father has done for the loving Son who has so well done His Father's will. May we, who offer our wills in loving imitation of Christ and together with His will, experience ever the same delights of soul.

COMMUNION – John 16:8.

This repeats the Gospel words: "When the Paraclete, the Spirit of truth, comes, He will prove the world wrong about sin and about rightness of heart and about judging." This is the first promise of the Holy Spirit in the Masses that follow Easter. See in the music the fluttering down of the Dove at *Cum venerit* and the settling down at *Paraclitus*.

Spiritus veritatis is exalted because truth must ever be. Note how completely *de peccato*, *de justitia*, and *de judicio* are phrased, as if to mark the difference in each: the first descends to the earth; there is a calmness about the second; the third seems to tell us that God alone is judge of the living and the dead—all judgment should be left to Him. May He who comes to us in holy Communion find us ever ready for His Holy Spirit, ever mindful of His judgment rather than that of the world! His presence alone can convince us of the value of possessing Him, who possesses all grace.

FIFTH SUNDAY AFTER EASTER

This Sunday is marked by a gladsome expression of joyful thanksgiving for the divine assistance that has come to us through redemption. While a quiet joy has marked each Sunday since Easter, today's is more of jubilation. We know that our Savior will soon leave earth to return to heaven, but we are not sad on that account; rather, we should like the whole world to know how much cause there is for rejoicing.

INTROIT – Isaias 48:20; Psalm 65:1-2.

"Speak with a voice full of joy, and let it be heard. Tell it even to the ends of the earth: the Lord has freed His people from the bondage of sin.—I will sing joyfully to You, O God, with all the earth. I will praise You with a psalm and will glorify Your holy Name." The first word should, no doubt, be "Shout."

The music begins mildly, as if to tell us our *jucunditatis* should rise from the earth and be a heavenly joy. Notice how quietly we come down to the last notes of *annuntiante*. But it must be more than just joy of heart; it must be a joy that will be heard (*audiatur*). See the extremes of the earth to which we must reach (*ad extremum terrae*). The *liberavit Dominus* is the most important news to be told. See, too, how being liberated has lifted up God's people, as is so well shown in the final notes of *populum suum*. Once more the *Jubilate* sings out its message, too. (The Introit for the feast of the Immaculate Conception was adapted from today's Introit. Do you see the resemblance in both the music and the thought?)

ALLELUIA

Holy Mother Church never tires of telling us that all we have in the way of grace rises from the triumph that followed Calvary. Today's first Alleluia verse stresses St. Paul's idea (1 *Cor*. 15, 20ff.): "The risen Christ, the first fruit of those who sleep, will cause to rise all those who belong to Him." "Christ is risen, and has let His light shine upon us, who have been redeemed at the price of His Blood."

The first *Alleluia* gives us a picture of the resurrection; and

74

repeating that music on the first two words makes the fact still more evident to us. In *et illuxit* see the glory of His having risen, shining down on us. In *redemit* there is happiness, because that is what we so prize. A tender note, almost one of sadness, is heard in *sanguine suo*, as we recall the price of our redemption.

In the second Alleluia verse (*John* 16:28)—"It was from the Father I came out when I entered the world, and now I am leaving the world and going on My way to the Father"—we strike repetition, but there seems to be a parallel: "I came out from the Father into the world; I go out from the world unto the Father." "The heights on *a Patre...veni...-quo mundum,* and *vado ad Patrem* are not of joy; they sound as if the composer wants to stress heaven through all this. There is a little sadness in the strain. It must have been difficult for our Lord to leave His eternal Father, to come down to earth; then to leave His apostles is another sadness for Him. We may counteract the effect, however, if we make the words *vado ad Patrem* our own. The anticipated joy we should feel at those words will make the music warm and heartfelt.

OFFERTORY – Psalm 65:8-9,20.

"May all nations bless You, O Lord, and make Your praise resound throughout the earth. Let them bless You for Your kindness to me, giving me a continued life in which to serve You and a steadfastness in Your service. May You be blessed, my Lord and my God, who did not turn away from my petition or stint Your mercy to me!" This adaptation by Abbot Smith is very good for us to make our own. However, the composer applied the words not so much to the souls who would be singing this Offertory as to our Lord.

Recall the words of the Easter Introit—Christ's words to the Eternal Father: "I have risen and am still with You. You have placed Your hand on me; how wonderful is Your knowledge." The music today seems to parallel that same idea, as though our Lord is quietly saying to His apostles, before He leaves them: "Now show your gratitude to My Father for all that He has done. Let Him hear your voice praising Him, He who has set My soul to live and has not turned away from My prayer in the Garden, as I thought at that time He had. He has shown, through

Me, how generous He can be with His mercy. So let Him hear your voices praising Him!"

The song itself is subdued but, realizing the full import of the words in both senses, the heart must be filled with an intense joy. The organist should play the melody softly, while you try to catch our Lord's voice saying those words. You will notice that, for the most part, the music is serious. Only at *posuit* and again at *suam* (near the end) does the voice rise to any height. Then, having made our own offertory, let us sing the words as our own. When we have sought to establish His reign in our own hearts, we can much more easily be imbued with the desire to see hearts all over the world, all nations, turning to Him in love.

COMMUNION – Psalm 95:2.

"I will praise You, O Lord, and my praise shall consist in the imitation of Your Son, my Lord, who manifests Your Name to men. My sincere praise of You, O my God, will be found in my efforts to apply to my soul day by day the salvation Your Son has purchased for me." This, our final song of exultation in today's Mass, is also a very beautiful one.

The melody of this Communion is very much like that of the Introit, making the picture of today's joy complete. Note also how the music of both *cantate*'s is the same, but the second *Domino* reaches a happier level. Note the reverence of the music again on *nomen ejus*. To the music on *bene*, sing "See how very good and becoming"; how well it emphasizes that *bene*! The *nuntiate* carries the picture of spreading out the news, just as does *diem* (day by day). There is great joy in the second last *alleluia*; the final one is a little more sedate.

This song should, indeed, be a happy one. Our Lord is in our hearts; we have just had a visit from Him. May our praise of Him ever hold the promise of the words we sing: not only to imitate Him, but each day to make the effort of applying more and more to our souls the salvation that our Guest has won for us. He will not be wanting with His help. In the Gospel today, He promises us that help: "Make your request of the Father in My Name, and He will grant it to you...."

ASCENSION THURSDAY

When our Lord first appeared on earth, God's angels announced to the shepherds that the Savior of the world was born in Bethlehem. Now as He goes back to the Father, angels again tell the news, this time of His ascension. The apostles are the ones to receive the message.

INTROIT – Acts 1:11; Psalm 46:2.

"Men of Galilee, why do you stand here looking heavenward? He who has been taken from you into heaven, this same Jesus, will come back in the same fashion, just as you have watched Him going into heaven.—Let all the earth rejoice with me, O Lord, as I raise my hands in prayer to You."

See the *Viri Galilaei* gazing up into heaven. The *quid admiramini* shows the admiration of the disciples, as *caelum* shows the heights to which our Lord has ascended. The same thought is found in the music of *ascendentem in caelum*; and *ita veniet* shows the promised return to earth. The joy that mingles both words with the music finds still further expression in the psalm verse.

When the Holy Father enters the Vatican for today's Mass, the people, in their enthusiasm, will clap their hands all the time he is passing through their midst. Even though today's greeting will be very great, it will be but a faint echo of the welcome that will be given to our Lord as He comes to us again at the end of the world.

ALLELUIA – Psalm 46:6; Psalm 67:18-19.

"You, my Lord, have ascended on high to prepare a place for me.—The Lord is in the midst of His saints, and in His Church and His tabernacle. You have ascended to heaven, O Lord, after Your victory, to find a place for Your captives of love." These verses carry out the thought of today's Introit.

Look at the Alleluia verse for the third Sunday of Advent and you will see that the music is the same. On that Advent Sunday we were getting close to our Lord's coming; today we are looking up to the place in the clouds where He vanished. The music of both *Alleluias* gives a splendid picture of the ascension. The repetition of the first one on *voce tubae* seems something like the silver trumpets that ring out during the Consecration in St. Peter's Basilica on this day. In the second part, *duxit* shows the captives of love being led to God—a pleasant *captivitatem* with the Victim of divine love.

OFFERTORY – Psalm 46:6.

"You, my Lord, have ascended on high to prepare a place for me." Although these words have just been sung in the Alleluia, here they are given to us in a new musical setting. See again the picture of the ascension in the first two words; and note the joyful melody of *jubilatione*, which is repeated on *Dominus*. The sound of the *voce tubae* now comes down from heaven to us, a signal of God's pleasure when we offer to ascend above the earth with Him.

COMMUNION – Psalm 67:33-34.

"I will sing to You, O Lord, ascending in Your glory as the sun rising in splendor." The music of *psallite Domino* is very sober and reverent, as if we are composing ourselves before prayer for the praise that is to follow.

Isn't it surprising that, although the same words or at least the same ideas, occur so often, the composer is able to find new ways of setting them to music, ways that truly adorn those expressions and bring out so much more clearly their import? In this Communion, *ascendit* does not reach the heights it does in other places, but we feel the uplift in the music of *super caelos*. It is not difficult to see the sunrise in the music of *Orientem*. The glory of sunrise is just past, as our Lord comes into our hearts in holy Communion; and we feel that we are ascending above the mundane earth with Him to the highest heavens. The final *alleluia* is expressive of our joyful thanksgiving.

SUNDAY AFTER ASCENSION

INTROIT — Psalm 26:7-9,1.

"O Lord, hear my voice; have mercy on me and listen to my prayer. My heart has promised You to see Your face, that I may know Your will. Turn not away Your face from me, nor go far away and leave me desolate, my kind, loving Lord.—You, O Lord, are the true Light that will shine upon me, and go before me to show me the way of my salvation. Why, then, should I fear?"

The music of the first word is like a call to attention; that of *Domine* reaches up to catch the Lord's ear. Except for that initial cry for notice, the music of this Introit is very simple, yet very tender. The words do not need any other kind of music, since they so well express the longing of the soul for the Spouse of the Church. We are quietly awaiting the promised Paraclete.

ALLELUIA — Psalm 46:9; John 14:18.

"O Lord, who can rule over all nations, come and rule over me, and make Your throne in my heart!—I will not leave you friendless: I go, but I am coming to you, and then your hearts will be glad." The music of the first *Alleluia* is almost sad; certainly it is not as bright as the normal run of *Alleluias*. However, it shakes off that first feeling, as we consider our Lord in heaven *super omnes gentes.*

The music on *Deus* shows God ruling over all mankind. Then, with God's throne established in our hearts, we rise joyfully in the second *Alleluia*, a very beautiful melody. The repetition of the first group of notes following the asterisk is particularly joyful, especially as it begins for the third time. There is a confident joy in the music on the word *Non*. And *vos* is very humble, as we consider that God has been mindful of us, His creatures still on earth. The music of *relinquam* seems to say that "even though our Lord has ascended into heaven, He is still not unmindful." The *vado* shows Him going to the eternal Father, and the *venio* truly pictures His coming to us again. The word *gaudebit* is especially joyful, since its music is borrowed from the glad *Alleluia* just sung. This joy should ever be in *cor vestrum.*

OFFERTORY — Psalm 46:6.

This is the same as the Offertory that we sang on Ascension Thursday. It adds the needed note of triumphant joy that our hearts expect.

COMMUNION — John 17:12-13,15.

"Father, as long as I was with them, it was for Me to keep them true to Your Name; but now I am coming to You. I am not asking that You take them out of the world, but that You keep them clear from what is evil." Note the deep reverence in the music on that word *Pater*. One can almost see Christ raising His eyes to heaven at *cum essem cum eis*. Then the *ego servabam* ...is a mere statement of fact.

At *nunc* there seems to be a change in the music, as there is in the thought. See how beautifully He seems to ascend at *ad te venio*. That phrase is the most beautiful in the whole song, both for the music and for the application by which we can make those words our own. God has just come into our hearts in holy Communion; exalted above all creatures of the earth, we promise *ad te venio*. Since Christ does not ask His Father to take us from the lowly *mundo* but to keep us from evil (*serves a malo*), we can let our joyful hearts thank Him in the *alleluia*.

PENTECOST

Pentecost is a foreign-mission feast par excellence. The Introit is not very clear in the Douay Bible or in most missals. Father Kent labored for a long time over this to give us the following translation:

INTROIT — Wisdom 1:7; Psalm 67:2.

"The Holy Spirit's presence pervades the whole earth, and He who created all things understands the capabilities that the human voice possesses." That is, the Spirit of the Lord is covering the whole world, waiting for missioners to go out to all men and, by their teachings, take that same divine Spirit to other souls.

In today's feast the reference is, of course, to that gift of the Holy Spirit which unloosed the tongues of the apostles and empowered them to tell "of the wonderful things of God." The enemies of the Church were not wanting in those days, nor have they been since that time. That is why the psalm verse sings: "God will arise in His might and put His enemies to flight; they who hate Him will flee before the spread and the growth of the Church that God has founded." The "spread and growth" are our work.

Just as the Christmas solemnity announced the nature of the feast by its first word, *Puer*, and Easter did the same with *Resurrexi*, so the first words of today's Introit tell us that it is the feast of *Spiritus Domini*. The music begins reverently, but very soon it reaches great heights as if the Dove is hovering on its wings all about the earth (*replevit orbem terrarum*). God's creation is portrayed in *et hoc...omnia*, and the heavenly message stands out in *scientiam habet vocis*. May our singing of this glorious Introit be a prayer that not only fills our hearts, but also sends echoes, like the Pentecostal flames, into the hearts of many of God's creatures over the world.

ALLELUIA -- Psalm 103:30.

"You sent forth Your Spirit, and new life was created in Your apostles. You clothed the whole face of the earth. Come, Holy Spirit, fill the hearts of those who love You, and let Your love ever burn in their hearts." In the Epistle we had the beautiful story of the Cenacle, and the marvelous effects that followed the visit of the Holy Spirit. Then that story is fittingly followed by this Alleluia.

The music of *Emitte* shows the Dove, loosed from heaven, hovering a little overhead and then coming down to those who have just finished their nine-day prayer. In *Spiritum tuum* we can almost see the Spirit touching each one of them separately. In *et creabuntur* is portrayed the rising new life that was imparted to the apostles, so that they would be able to go far abroad and renew the earth (*faciem terrae*). The first *Alleluia* is not unfamiliar to us; we met it for the first time on Gaudete Sunday, where we asked God to show His power and come and save us. Again, on the second Sunday after Epiphany, we asked angelic spirits to join us in praising God for having manifested Himself to the nations. Then more recently, as our Lord ascended to heaven, we sang this same melody as a prelude to what we expected and hoped and prayed for: today's realization.

With the full force of that realization upon us, we drop to our knees in holy expectancy. (The rubrics tell us: "Here all kneel.") Note the invitation contained in the music of *Veni,* as though we are saying, "Do come down upon all of us here!" Then our souls rise to Him who lifts them in love, *Sancte Spiritus.* The music of *reple...fidelium* is a plea to "make our love like to Thine." What an exalted picture the composer paints of that love in *tui amoris,* reaching so devotionally, so harmoniously, so tenderly to such great heights! In *eis ignem* we see the effect of His breath blowing on the dying embers of our hearts, fanning them into a great flame of love.

What a great feast it could be for us today if, by these our prayers, we could help the people of all nations to know the gift that might be theirs if they would turn in love to God! One of the best ways to make that prayer effective is to be sure that our own love today is above reproach. "Between love and love, there is nought but love!" If our longing for the pure, deep, faithful, enrapturing love of the Holy Spirit is ever increasing, we shall sing these chants today with all the deep fervor with which they have been sung through centuries since the composer first presented them, with the same loving ardor with which our Lady called upon the Paraclete during her Pentecostal novena.

SEQUENCE

A literal translation may help us to sing the familiar music reverently and fervently, as we recall our own needs and as we grow in sympathetic union with all human beings who are our brothers:

Come, Holy Spirit, and send forth from heaven a ray of your light.

Come, Father of the poor; come, Giver of gifts; come, Light of the world.

You are the best consoler, sweet guest of the soul, sweet cooling breeze; in labor, our rest; in heat, our relief; in tears, our solace.

O most blessed Light, fill the most hidden recesses of our hearts.

Without Your help divine, there is nothing in man, nothing but what is hurtful.

Wash what is sordid in us; refresh our aridity; heal the wounds of our souls; bend our stubborn wills; warm our coldness; guide us aright when we would go astray.

Give to Your faithful ones who confide in You, Your seven great gifts; help us to merit virtue; make safe our going forth from this life, that we may be worthy of Your gift of eternal happiness.

We shall better understand the words of the Gospel after the Holy Spirit has enlightened us to see the underlying principle of love and has moved us to be more thoughtful of the Father's will. Then it will be easier to cast self aside, easier to overcome selfish wills and offer ourselves without reserve to the God of Love. So we shall sing our offering.

OFFERTORY — Psalm 67:29-30.

"Make content, O God, the hearts You have chosen for Your grace. Accept the offerings that kings bring to You for Your temple and the adornment of Your tabernacle."

The music of *Confirma* seems to say: "Make us constant by lifting us up to Thee, O God." Then *hoc* seems to give promise of great things to come, and it is followed reverently by *Deus*, reminding us that all good things come from God. At *operatus es in nobis*, see how we are exalted when God works in and through us, His temples in this world (*a templo...in Jerusalem*). The offerings that kings brought for the adornment of the temple are beautifully pictured in *tibi...munera*. Our offerings at the Offertory will be just as acceptable when we offer the best that we have, and the temples of the Holy Spirit will be come beautiful by our gifts. We are of the royalty, we who are the temples!

COMMUNION — Acts 2:2,4.

"All at once a sound came from heaven, like that of a strong wind blowing, and filled the whole house where they were sitting; and they were filled with the Holy Spirit and began to tell of God's wonders."

The music from *Factus* to *Spiritu Sancto* is all of one piece, like the wind gathering momentum and carrying things swiftly along. Picture a light piece of paper caught up by the wind, high above our heads, with only one or two little swoops downward. That music should be sung at a good tempo, but as easily as the wind should carry the paper along. At *magnalia Dei* the music changes to reverential awe and ends with the prayerfully thoughtful *alleluia*. It is our song of thanksgiving, not only for the coming of the Holy Spirit into our hearts, but also for the gift of Eucharistic love that is ours. The miracle of the first Pentecost is always ours in holy Communion: in the form of bread God comes into our hearts, and His gifts stay with us as long as our wills remain united to the will of Jesus, one with the eternal Father.

TRINITY SUNDAY

The melody of today's Introit is not unfamiliar. We met it on the first Sunday of Lent and have used it in votive Masses of thanksgiving. The motif of the whole feast is contained herein and beautifully expressed in the words.

INTROIT – Tobias 12:6; Psalm 8:2.

"Blessed be the Holy Trinity and undivided Unity. We will give glory to the Triune God, because He has shown His mercy to us.—O Lord, my God, how great and glorious You are in the whole earth! Would that I could appreciate the glory of the Father, of the Son, and of the Holy Spirit."

See the ascent and descent on the first two words. We raise our hearts and hands to praise and bless God, and immediately His blessings come down upon us. The same picture of our offering and His return is contained in *sancta...unitas*, and again in *confitebimur ei*, where our expression of faith in the mystery reaches to heaven. The *quia* is our reason: because He has made known to us how merciful He can be. The continued rise and fall of the music is very impressive from this point of view, as if to assure us that blessings will follow if we bow our heads and pray:

"O Triune God, I do not understand this mystery, but I do not ask to understand anything. Only give me always the faith to believe what You have told me is true, that which You have proved to me by the numberless blessings bestowed upon me each

time I raise my heart and hands to You. Greater minds than mine
have bowed their heads, confessing their faith in Father, Son,
and Holy Spirit, Three in One; and because of their faith, You
have given them insight into still greater mysteries. Let me believe with Origen, Justin, Jerome, Augustine, Aquinas. Although
my words of praise may never reach their sublime heights, I may
believe as deeply, and be blessed as abundantly as were they."

GRADUAL – Daniel 3:55-56.

"Blessed art Thou, O Lord, who looks deeply into the abyss
of our nothingness and who are enthroned above the angels.
Blessed are Thou in heaven, O Lord, and worthy of praise through
every age." In this Gradual, the feeling of the Introit music is repeated in the opening words. The singer of the divine mysteries
cuts short the blessings of *es* to sing his wonder in *Domine*.

Qui intueris shows God looking down from the heights of
heaven into the abyss of our nothingness; He who is enthroned
above the Cherubim is easily pictured in *sedes super Cherubim*.
The "*sursum corda*" of the second *Benedictus es* is interrupted
again by the singer to express his wonderful admiration of the
Name of God in *Domine*. In *firmamento coeli* he expresses the
devotion of all creation, both heaven and earth. And *laudabilis
in saecula* repeats again the thought of the Introit: our praise and
love of God, when expressed and proved by our love, come back
to us in love and blessings beyond all comparison.

ALLELUIA – Daniel 3:52.

"You are blessed, O Lord, God of our fathers; may You be
praised by Your creatures through all ages."

The music of the Alleluia verse emphasizes not only God's
love for us, but also His infinite splendor. As the Fathers of the
Church through all ages have praised and blessed the Blessed
Trinity, may it be given to us, too, in our poor, feeble way, to
sing of the blessings that have been ours all through life, blessings that may be ours for all eternity, as we sing the never-ending
alleluias of His praise.

OFFERTORY – Tobias 12:6.

"Blessed be God the Father, and His only-begotten Son, together with the Holy Spirit, because He has made known His

mercy to us!" See in the procession of notes the great concourse of souls who have, from the beginning, come to offer themselves at the Offertory of the holy Sacrifice. Theirs are countless hands and hearts raised to God, forgetful of self, and acknowledging that all they have has come to them from God.

So in our poor offering of self we really have nothing that is our own to give. We can only give back to the Father, who created us; to the Son, who lovingly redeemed us; to the Holy Spirit, who taught us how to love only the treasures that came from Their hands to us. Notice that the highest notes of the music are concerned with the Father, and that those we sing of the Son and the Holy Spirit are but a fraction removed for the most part, although in one instance they do reach the same heights. See, too, their blessings coming down to us in *misericordiam suam*. Has not that always been our experience in the holy Sacrifice? The greater lengths we went to in offering ourselves and all we have to God, the greater by far has been God's return to us.

COMMUNION — Tobias 12:6.

"We bless the Lord of heaven and profess before all creation our faith in Him, and then we are showered with His benefits." This fulfills the thought stated at the close of comments on today's Offertory: We can give back to God only what has already come to us from Him.

In *et coram omnibus* is our open expression of faith, and the music from *confitebimur* to *suam* seems to show God continually stooping down with His gifts to us. O admirable exchange! Our sacrificial gifts, consecrated and made one with the Sacrifice of Christ, come back to us in the whole gift of Him whom the heavens cannot contain. Thanks unendingly to You, O Blessed Trinity, who teach, inspire, and reward us with such great tokens of Your loving gratitude for our poor expressions of love!

CORPUS CHRISTI

INTROIT – Psalm 80:17,2.

"You would have fed them with the choicest bread, O God, and with the sweetest honey, and with that food they would have been fully satisfied."—"I will rejoice before You, my God, my only Helper. I will sing unto You, for You are my God."

There is great joy in the music today. The melodies are familiar to us; we have sung them often. The opening music pictures God stooping down to earth to pluck the wheat from which the bread is made, in order that He might nourish our souls with His food. Has He not actually stooped down from heaven, too, to lift us more surely to Himself through the sacrament of holy Eucharist? The *petra melle* is of heaven, too, as is *saturavit*. But the sweetness of honey is insipid compared to that of our heavenly Manna. The only real satiety of soul that can be found is in heaven, whence comes this "Food of Angels." Can you for even a moment imagine what religion would be without the Blessed Sacrament? No wonder our psalm is *Jubilate Deo!* May our every song be one of joy for this great boon that is ours.

GRADUAL – Psalm 144:15-16.

"My eyes shall hope in You, O my God, that You will give me consolation in Your own good time. In Your hands are blessings for us all, and You supply the wants of every living creature." We say these words of the Gradual every day in our grace before meals. How fittingly these same words are applied to our daily supernatural nourishment!

Oculi omnium are our eyes of the lower earth, raised toward heaven, waiting, hoping. A little ascent begins on *in te sperant*, as our hopes rise, too, for we realize that the Lord will provide. Note once more how the saintly composer expresses his love for God's Name in *Domine*. Then *et tu das illis escam* shows the gifts, heavenly gifts, coming down to us, to even the very lowliest of the earth. Abbot Smith translates *in tempore opportuno* as "in God's good time." The music on those words shows us that God will constantly, at all times, supply the food of our souls, if we but hold ourselves ready to receive it.

The music from *Aperis* to *benedictione* gives us a fine picture
of the graces that come down from heaven to the souls of all
men, raising us to heaven in order that we may ever remember
that we of the earth (*omne animal*) are all one, united in the one
common Food that is given us from the altar. When I receive
Communion, I must never forget that the poor, unkempt, home-
less man receiving next to me is one with me, my brother, in the
Food that our common Father gives us. Each day we should say,
"I am one with every soul in the world who is receiving Communion today!"

ALLELUIA — John 6:56-57.

"My Flesh is real food, My Blood is real drink. He who
eats My Flesh and drinks My Blood lives continually in Me,
and I live in him." The music for this Alleluia is very joyful,
reaching sublime heights. It should be sung quickly and lightly,
but with the correct rhythm and accent; no part of the music
should be slurred over merely to keep it light.

The rise and fall of the music on *Caro mea vere est cibus*
seems like the natural accents of our Lord's voice as He first
said those words. No great height is yet reached in the music,
perhaps because food is a mundane thing. But at *sanguis...est
potus*, see to what heights we ascend! It is as if our Lord is saying:
"My food will nourish your soul in spiritual growth while you
are still on earth. But it was by shedding My Blood for you that
I opened the door of heaven, where, if you are faithful, you will
have no need of nourishment, but will have the actuality of eternal
life with Me." That thought carries us through the next words to
manet. Then *et ego in eo* pictures for us, more vividly than any
words, the greatness of the promise that is made, the condescension of God coming down from heaven to the tabernacle to en-
close Himself in our hearts. The singing of that final *-o* in *eo* has
always sounded like the breathless awe of a child who stands
enraptured before some great sight. Oh, the beauty, the mystery
of God coming in love into such a cluttered heart as mine!

SEQUENCE

This glorious song of today's Mass is too little known. It
has been called the shortest, most comprehensive teaching of the

entire dogma of the holy Eucharist. Note, for example, verse 7: "In the new King's banquet, in the New Law's new oblation, ends the ancient paschal rite"; and verse 9: "What He did at supper seated, Christ enjoined to be repeated, when His love we celebrate"; and verse 10: "Thus obeying His orders, bread and wine of our salvation, we the victim consecrate"; and verse 11: "Tis for Christian faith asserted, bread is into Flesh converted, into Blood the holy wine: sight and intellect transcending, nature's law to marvel bending, 'tis confirmed by faith divine."

I once read that the Benedictine monks at Beuron sing this Sequence in six minutes. That could be a guide to the tempo in which it might be sung. The music of the entire hymn is very expressive. In the twenty-second verse, the music of *datur manna patribus* shows the manna falling from heaven in the desert.

OFFERTORY – Lev. 21:6.

"The priests of the Lord offer incense to the Lord, and bread, and so stand blessed before God, honoring His holy Name." *Sacerdotes* shows priests lifted up between the earth and heaven by their ordination, reminding us that they stand a little above us and a little below God as intermediaries between God and man.

Note again the devotional music on *Domini*. In *incensum* there is a picture of the wisps of smoke rising from the censer; and in *panes* one can almost see the loaves neatly piled on the altar of sacrifice. The *offerunt* shows the heights to which the poor offertory of our wills should reach. The continual rise and fall of the music is indicative of the motif we considered on Trinity Sunday: whatever our offering may be, no matter how worthless it may seem in the eyes of the world, if it is given because of our love it will bring back gifts out of all proportion to our puny sacrifices. We offer all we have, all we are; but, naturally, this means that sin must be excluded. The music of *non polluent nomen eius* amplifies that thought.

COMMUNION – 1 Corinthians 11:26-27.

"Whenever you eat this bread and drink this cup, you are heralding the Lord's death, until He comes; and therefore, if anyone eats this bread or drinks this cup of the Lord unworthily, he will be held to account for the Lord's Body and Blood." Who could blame us if we were to shout the beautiful music for these words?

The music is that of *Factus*, which we sang on Pentecost. There is a suitable similarity in the words: on Pentecost we sang of the Holy Spirit filling our hearts; today we sing of the *Panis angelicus*. Yet, we could not partake of the Eucharist had not the Holy Spirit opened the doors of our hearts and planted therein the germ of love. The music of the Communion verse is, for the most part, simply expressive of the words. It has all the directness that the words of St. Paul usually have. The final words of the Communion seem very serious, but they are softened by the simple melody of the final *Alleluia*.

As every day is Christmas and Good Friday, too, how fortunate we are that every day for us is also the commemoration of Corpus Christi. May our love of the holy Sacrifice, and our share in it each day, help us to reap the harvest of the oblation in the holy Eucharist with hearts ever grateful for the sublime privilege that is ours. *Futurae gloriae nobis pignus datur.*

SUNDAY AFTER CORPUS CHRISTI

Note: Although the following text was written for those who have been favored with a religious vocation, it may, nevertheless, serve to provide a better understanding, if not an incentive, to those choristers who have not been called to such a life.

Abbot Smith's paraphrase of the psalms used in today's liturgy gives us a picture of our very life in the cloister, the convent, or the seminary. Each separate song, from the Introit to the Communion, makes a complete subject worthy of considerable meditation.

INTROIT — Psalm 17:19-20,2-3.

"After many falls, owing to my willfulness, You, my God, have become my protector. You have shown kindness in so many ways. You have brought me into an open space, that is, into the free air of religion, and have saved me from the world because You were pleased with me, since I have determined to stay near Your Son, in whom You are well pleased."—"My love shall be fixed on You, my God, for You are my only strength, enabling me to persevere in the vocation You have given me. You surround me as a firmament; You are my refuge in all the trials of life, my protection in each temptation."

The music of *Factus est* pictures our calling from the earthiness of the world to serve God; and the music of *Dominus* follows the reverent pattern usual for the mention of the Lord's Name. Then *protector meus* seems to indicate the steps by which we were led to God—*eduxit*; and *in latitudinem* portrays the "free air of religion" into which we were lifted from the earth. The great heights of such a vocation make us more mindful of the need we have of God's continued protection; and so we are humbled at *salvum me fecit*, but encouraged to look up to God, continually, asking Him to lift us up to Him—*quoniam voluit*.

GRADUAL – Psalm 119:1-2.

"At the very entrance of my religious life, I was in trouble, for You, my God, would not let me settle down in the world. I cried to You and You heard me. As soon as I felt the first impulse to the cloister, I had to hear much from wicked lips against the life I desired; and from deceitful tongues I heard much that made me fear to take the step."

Thus is continued the meditation on our vocation. Note the reverent awe and timidity with which we enter religion, as expressed in *Ad Dominum*. It is to God we hasten for protection in our difficulty on leaving the world—*cum tribularer*. You will catch the ululation of our cry if you sing the *clamavi* music on the syllable *oo*. The joy of finally reaching God's ear and having been heard is well expressed in *exaudivit me*; the confidence of a soul knowing that he may expect God's help is shown in the music of *Domine*. There is a plaintive cry in *libera*; and *anima mea* shows the depths to which the soul has fallen. Then *a labiis iniquis* shows the battle in which some souls must engage before they are able to tear themselves from the world and give themselves to God; and *lingua dolosa* is very expressive of the sadness experienced.

ALLELUIA — Psalm 7:2.

"In all the difficulties and trials of life, I must hope for help from You, O my God! By Your power alone can I be secure." The thought of the Gradual is repeated in this Alleluia.

There is a fine expression of faith in God's hearing our song, as expressed in the music of *Domine, Deus meus, in te speravi,* and the repetition of the same strain in *salvum me fac.* At *libera me* the cry of the soul reaches to its greatest heights; and in the final music we can even picture God looking kindly down, assuring us of security and of the protection of grace that He will place around us.

OFFERTORY — Psalm 6:5.

"I will remember You at all times as my Savior and my merciful Redeemer. I will entreat You to snatch my soul from all infidelity." This is a quiet, grateful prayer and promise of a soul that has found peace and security in God's service.

The music for this Offertory is one of the simplest melodies to be found. You can easily sing it at a glance. The *fah-sol* repetition is by no means tiring or tiresome; it seems to express perfectly the equanimity of soul that comes from having "put on Christ." Our personal offertory has united us to Christ in a very special manner; there is no further cause for disturbance. While we remain one with Him in all things, we are leading a well-balanced life.

COMMUNION — Psalm 12:6.

"I will sing to Your Name, O my God, my own Lord, in whom I place all my trust." Here we sing of the joy that fills our souls because of the great Gift that has come to us.

The *cantabo* is a song of itself, leading us to the reverent melody of *Domino.* See the "good" that God has given us, so beautifully expressed in the music of *qui bona tribuit mihi.* Then when the thought of God's Treasure now within us reminds us of the great wealth of riches we have received, our voices soar aloft in a psalm of great beauty, praising the Name of the most high God.

Our vocation alone would be cause enough for the greatest degree of gratitude, but we have received much more. We accepted the invitation to "come, follow" Him, and from that moment we began a new, heavenly bank account of blessings and graces. In our vocation we accepted Christ's invitation, and God rewarded us. In the holy Sacrifice Christ bids us to be one with Him in offering our wills to the eternal Father; and for that great privilege the Father gives us back His Son in holy Communion. No wonder we sing! May we so recognize God's benefits to us each new day that psalms of purest joy will ever be on our lips, to thank and praise Him always.

SACRED HEART

This feast of love should serve as a reminder of the extent to which God's love went, searching us out, wheedling us away from the things that spelled danger to our souls, and back to His Sacred Heart. Who can measure the extent of that love? As we sing the Introit of today's Mass, let our hearts be firm in the promises we make; let the joy of our singing be indicative of our happiness in being so favored as to be apostles of the Sacred Heart, heralds of His love.

INTROIT – Psalm 32:11,19,1.

"I will listen to Your words alone, O Lord, and the whisperings of Your heart I will be careful to hear forever. Then You will deliver me from sin and will encourage me in the time of desolation.—In my striving after perfection, I must not be downhearted, but joyful, in Your service, O Lord."

In the music, *Cogitationes* shows our thoughts arising to God, and *Cordis ejus* seems to indicate His making those thoughts of His known to us, sent down to earth to us. The next phrase indicates something of the length to which God has gone to let us know of His love. Clearly *ut eruat* portrays the act of raising from the dead (the state of sin) the soul of man, who prefers to cling to earthiness rather than to be lifted to God.

Soon *et alat* pictures the same idea, as if God says: "No matter how often men turn away from Me, how much they stop loving Me, I will never stop loving them, never cease trying in My love to draw their hearts back to Me. I will love them always

with an everlasting love. Perhaps, some day, My plea of love will
penetrate through the pall that worldliness casts about My beloved ones, and they will again turn to Me in love."

GRADUAL – Psalm 24:8-9.

Abbot Smith's paraphrase follows the above-stated idea.
"You are always kind to me, O my God, and so full of desire
for my keeping in Your love, that You do not stop loving sinners who have left Your way. How much more interest do You
take in leading the meek of heart to the heights of perfection!
You manifest to such the secrets of Your love."

The sweetness of *dulcis* is shown in the music in a very clear
way. In *et rectus* our eyes and thoughts are lifted to the beauty
of the Sacred Heart; *Dominus* has the great reverence always reserved for God's Name. The Law being given on Mount Sinai
is pictured in *legem dabit delinquentibus*; it is the law of love, and
in via shows it coming down through the ages to all men. *Diriget*
is a trumpet call, bidding us to look up and see how gently God
lifts us up to Him; then *docebit* tells us how much of heaven there
is in God's words to us, if we will but heed them. We find in *mites*
and *vias suas* beautiful pictures of the humility of Christ, begging
us to follow His humble example. He came down to earth, to
become a man like other men, to live on earth. He abased Himself to the lowest possible state, taking the form of a servant, so
that He might show us that our way of life is known to Him.

ALLELUIA – Matthew 11:29.

"Take My yoke upon yourselves, and learn from Me: I am
meek and humble of heart, and you shall find rest for your souls."
Here Christ seems to say to us: "As I rose above the earth by
doing the will of My Father, so too can you rise above yourselves
and keep your eyes and your hearts ever set on that one sign-
post: The Father's Will!"

The music of *Tollite jugem meum* looks like a yoke going
around the shoulders of two people. A yoke is made for two—our
Lord and myself; no one wears a yoke alone. In *et discite a me*,
we find the idea of our Lord's saying, "Let the sight of My loving
heart come down and touch your own heart with love." Then
see how humbly He passes over the word *mitis sum*, as if gentle-

ness is nothing of itself. It is great—reaching to God time and
again—only when it is founded upon the humility that is learned
in the school of the Sacred Heart. The assured rest to be found in
God, throughout a long eternity, is portrayed in *et invenietis*....
See how aptly the joy of the *Alleluia* follows that unerring promise!
OFFERTORY – Psalm 68:21.

Your divine Son, O Lord, when on the Cross, cried out:
"My heart expected reproach and misery, and I looked for one
who would grieve with Me, but there was none; for one who
would comfort Me, but I found him not." In this Offertory we
are shown how great a claim God has on us, urging us to make
the offerings of our hearts and wills one with His.

Except for the first word, all the music of the Offertory gives
the impression of our Lord's arms extended on the Cross—loving arms, reaching out to embrace the world but meeting no response. There is sadness in the music: a cry that goes into heaven.
The bitter disappointment is most poignantly expressed in the
high note on *non*. Who, after singing or hearing this cry from the
heart of Christ, could ever again deny Him the gift of love
for which He longs so ardently?
COMMUNION – John 19:34.

"One of the soldiers opened His side with a spear, and immediately blood and water flowed out." For almost the first time,
the Communion verse is not a song of thanksgiving; rather, it is
further proof of what eternal Love suffered to draw our hearts
to His. *Unus militum* is almost severe in the music, showing the
ruthlessness of those who wound our Lord. The next words,
lancea latus ejus aperuit, seem to give us a picture of the action
involved: the spear, drawn from its sheath and raised upward until it tore open the side of Calvary's Victim.

"On the Cross, His divinity lies hidden," says St. Thomas
Aquinas, and the blood and water flowing (*continuo exivit sanguis
et aqua*) portray the sacred humanity fully revealed. "In the Eucharist, Thy manhood is hidden," and we are at a divine banquet,
in quo Christus sumitur—the divine Christ. May He who took
upon Himself our humanity keep us ever worthy to taste of His
divinity, through our never-failing love and our devotion to the
love that shines forth from His great heart of love.

THIRD SUNDAY AFTER PENTECOST

We learned from the feast of the Sacred Heart the lesson our Lord taught: "Learn from Me; I am gentle and humble of heart; and you shall find rest for your souls." The liturgy of today's Mass and Office has us speaking of ourselves, as if we have learned well that lesson. The motif of today's Mass is to be found in the first Epistle of St. Peter (6:5): "Bow down, then, before the strong hand of God; He will raise you up, when His time comes to deliver you. Throw back on Him the burden of all your anxiety; He is concerned for you." Encouraged by this advice, we begin our day.

INTROIT – Psalm 24:16-18,1-2.

"Look kindly upon me, O Lord, and have great mercy on me, for without You I am alone and very poor. I will not try to hide my lowliness from You, or the trouble I have to keep in the right way; but I will ask You, my kind Lord, to forgive me all my sins.—To You, O Lord, I lift up my soul. I beg of You to give me this great grace: that I may be able at all times to lift my soul to You. You alone, Lord, can save me from the shame of forgetting You."

While the music of *Respice in me* is like a very timid plea for attention, it also reminds us of the Introit of the Mass for the dead—*Requiem*. There is room for much thought in comparing the two. When our own *Requiem* is being chanted over us, the degree of our "rest" in God will be in proportion to our having called upon Him in life to look at our souls, and to help us keep them in His humility. In *et miserere mei* is a plea to lift us up from our sins. The reverence of *Domine* is also expressive of great faith, as if to say, "I am sure that God's mercy will come down to my need, as long as I keep close to my Lord and Master."

See the frightened child alone and in the dark, crying out to his Father, in the music of *unicus et pauper sum ego*. Alone, and poor as I am in virtue, I can do nothing; but my eternal Father, seeing my need, can help me to rise if I sincerely cultivate *humilitatem meam*. I used to think that the exultant notes of those two words sounded like my friend who often asked, "Have you noticed how very humble I am?" In this instance, however, we are

96

merely confessing that, if we have been able to reach any degree of humility, it is because God has shown us the way. He knows better than we just how truly humble we are; the truth cannot be hidden from Him. There is a sad note in *laborem meum*, expressive of the trouble we have in trying to keep our souls lifted from the earth to God. The music of *et dimitte omnia peccata mea* is very humble, as it should be; but the soul rises again at *Deus meus*, in the realization that only God can forgive and teach us how to forgive.

GRADUAL – Psalm 54:23,17,19.

"I will put all my trust in You, O my Lord, and You will support and nourish my soul. I have cried unto You, O my God, and You will save me from all who fight against me and try to disturb me." This follows resolutely on St. Peter's advice. *Jacta* is very expressive of the act of casting ourselves on our knees before God, but *cogitatum tuum* shows us that our thoughts must be at all times with God (*in Domino*). Only then does His blessing come down on us, as expressed in the music of *te*. See, in *enutriet*, how God reaches down to earth to take the wheat of the field that is to become Food for our souls; how He takes It to heaven after consecration, and then hands It back to us for our nourishment. The music of our cry reaching to God is beautifully expressed in *clamarem ad Dominum*. We are confident that He will hear us—in the music of *exaudivit vocem meam*—and that from heaven He will protect me; He will stoop down to me and be with me, as I descend lower and lower in my efforts to lift myself to Him.

ALLELUIA – Psalm 7:12.

"How patient You have been with my waywardness in the past, O Lord! Grant that I may appease Your just anger by a more generous carefulness in my service from now on." There are holy fear and reverence in the music of *Deus judex justus*, as we think of the Last Judgment; but we are encouraged at *fortis et patiens* to remember that God's justice is ever tempered with mercy; and we rise hopefully in the final strains of the music, anticipating the rewarding *Alleluia* that we may one day be priviledged to sing before His Face.

OFFERTORY – Psalm 9:11-13.

Here we raise our hands and our hearts, with our offering of self, and the very act lifts us above the world. "I will trust You, O Lord, for You have shown Your kindness to me, allowing me to call You mine. May I, in seeking You, ever find You, O Lord! I will sing to Your Name and try to make known Your ways by my prayers and my faithful service. The trials of Your friends are always before You, O Lord. You do not turn aside from the cry of those who are poor in spirit."

The music for most of this beautiful song is exalted. The first strains, from *Sperent* to *Domine*, are of the highest; in no other place do strains reach these heights. This is as if to assure us that all who know God's holy Name, and who hope in Him because of that knowledge, are already blessed on earth. To catch the real beauty of the music on *Domine*, sing to those notes the words: "My Lord, my God, my All!"

In the next phrase, see the soul searching for God (*quaerentes*) and having found Him, lifting the heart to Him in the singing of this psalm. The singing (*psallite Domino*) should be by all, of high station or low, who dwell in the Sion of God's holy places. See, too, our poor prayers (*orationem pauperum*) rising to Him with our poor offerings, all that we have of self. How fortunate it is for us that God does not look at the value of our gifts, but considers rather the wealth of love with which they are given!

COMMUNION – Luke 15:10.

"I tell you, with the angels of God there is joy among them over one sinner that repents." Here we have our Lord Himself speaking to us. When you sing this simple melody, try to hear the tones of our Lord's voice as He first said these words. They carry the promise of the joy that awaits us if we work out our salvation in a humble, penitential way of life. Our joy of soul in just having received the Lord who said these words is but the foretaste of the *praemium* that is, God willing, to be ours some day because we have learned to "bow down before the Lord."

FOURTH SUNDAY AFTER PENTECOST

Today is another "vocation Sunday." The scene is set in the Gospel with the picture of Peter, James, and John leaving their nets and all things to follow Jesus. We, too, have left all things to follow Christ. We know that that following must be along the way of the Cross. For following that way, St. Paul, in his Epistle to the Romans, gives us the necessary guidance: "I count these present sufferings not as the measure of the glory that is to be revealed in us...while we await that adoption which is the ransoming of our bodies through Christ Jesus our Lord."

INTROIT – Psalm 26:1-3.

As we consider the above-stated background, the Introit is significant: "O Lord, You are the true light that will show me the way of my salvation. Why, then, should I fear? You, my Lord, will protect me from all evil if I am faithful to You, and You will help me to live my life in all protection.—I will have courage and not be cast down, even if whole armies assail me."

This music was met in the Introit on the Sunday after Epiphany. There is a bond between that "Light to the revelation of the Gentiles" and today's Introit. *Dominus* is a reverent lifting up of our hearts. (See also the Introit for the sixth Sunday after Pentecost.) Almost parallel are the passages for *illuminatio et salus mea*, although the second one reaches to the next highest note. There is evidence of strong faith in *quem timebo*. Note the similarity between the next *Dominus* and the first one. Using the same notes on *meae* (in reversed order) seems to give finality to the thought in that one place. Then the question that follows is a little bolder, since we have proclaimed God to be the defender of our lives. Faith and confidence carry us from *tribulant* through the paths of our enemies; and even under *infirmati* we do not waver. The last verse is fearlessly confident, too.

GRADUAL – Psalm 78:9-10.

"For the sake of Your holy Name, O Lord, forgive me my sins. Have not my enemies pointed to me as if I had no knowledge of You? Help me, O God, my Savior, and for the glory of Your Name, deliver me." It is only natural that the thought of past infidelities should make us give our whole allegiance to God. Perhaps we should say it is more than natural, it is above nature, supernatural. So we sing as in this Gradual.

The music of *Propitius esto* is humble, as we should be before the beauty of *Domine*. The music of *peccatis nostris* reminds us that our sins reached up in their malice to offend Heaven itself. The question of *ubi est* is very well depicted in that music. *Adjuva nos* begins very humbly, as did *propitius*; but, as soon as we realize that our salvation comes from God, our song reaches up to Him in great happiness. Hear the great honor in the music of *propter honorem*, and the whispered reverence in that unusual music for *nominis tui Domine*. Then the *libera nos* has the quiet assurance that comes to those who hold God's Name in holiness.

ALLELUIA – Psalm 9:5, 10.

"I will commit my cause to You, my Judge, who judges my intentions. I come to You as one so poor that I can do nothing for myself." On the word *Deus* the music is again very reverent, and *qui sedes* pictures God enthroned on high. *Super thronum* is another beautiful picture of the Providence of God spread out over the whole world, as God waits and is ready to show mercy to His beloved ones. The final notes echoing the *Alleluia* are happily descriptive of the mercy that all may expect who claim nothing for themselves, but rely unfailingly on His goodness.

OFFERTORY – Psalm 12:4-5.

"Enlighten my eyes O Lord, that I may be ever on the watch; let me not fall into the sleep that is the death of the soul, lest my enemy say that he has indeed prevailed against me." Here we come with hands laden, ready to give all that we have, in order that we may empty ourselves of all things and follow our vocation more surely with our Lord. The prayer that we should make our own is beautifully expressed in this Offertory.

The music of *Illumina* is like the first arousement of soul that should be ours in every Offertory. Then *oculos meos* are lifted to heaven. In that light we are able to see the depths to which the *obdormiam* of forgetfulness, the *morte* of sin, and the *inimicus meus* of earthly attachment can bring us. These three phases of detriment to our vocation are expressed in music that is similar.

The composer introduced a new strain, however, in *Praevalui adversus eum*, as if to remind us that, although our "enemy, the devil, goes about like a roaring lion, seeking his prey," we may defeat his purpose through a firm faith, keeping our eyes on God. No matter how low we may seem to be brought by trial, we receive enough reciprocating grace from the offering of ourselves to raise our eyes in confidence, in hope, to God.

COMMUNION – Psalm 17:3.

The truth stated above is the reason why, after receiving the Giver of all good gifts in holy Communion, we can say: "You are my only strength, my God, enabling me to persevere in the vocation You have given me. You surround me as a firmament. You are my refuge in all the trials of life, my protection in all temptation."

All the music of this beautiful song is like a hymn of thanksgiving. In *Dominus* we have the descent of the Lord of heaven into our hearts—the firm basis (*firmamentum*) that we need for our spiritual life. The humble admission that we have made of our need of Him is rewarded by our being lifted to a place of refuge (*refugium*) in His sacred Heart. Freed from our entanglement with the earth, we are elevated by our *Liberator*, God, *Deus meus*, who has deigned to come down to us. There is great gratitude expressed in the music of *adjutor meus*. Can we ever thank God enough for all that He has done for us?

FIFTH SUNDAY AFTER PENTECOST

The motif of today's liturgy seems to be found in this thought: "They who obey God's laws, by their evidence of love toward God and neighbor, will be given all the delights of soul that are necessary to keep heart, mind, and will one with God's." The humble realization that, without God's help, we could never reach such great heights, is first expressed in the Introit.

INTROIT – Psalm 26:7,9,1.

"O Lord, hear my voice; have mercy on me and listen to my prayer. You are my only hope, my only helper. Do not leave me, and in Your mercy do not despise me, for to whom can I go if You desert me?—You, O Lord, are the true Light that will shine upon me and show me the way of salvation. Why, then, should I fear?"

Note how the music of *Exaudi, Domine* is a bending down on the part of God, not only to regard our lowliness, but also to incline His ear to *vocem meam*, which tries to reach up to Him. We are abased at *qua clamavi ad te*, because we realize how little need there has been in the past to attend to our cry: too often we were self-reliant and failed to call upon Him. Note that *adjutor meus* seems to be a cry: "Attend to me doubly now. Let my prayer for Your continued help reach up to You." The *ne derelinquas me* and the *neque* cry earnestly but humbly. Then hear the reverence and unpresuming faith in *Deus, salutaris meus.*

This first part of the Introit could be paraphrased, according to the music: "I know I have not called upon You, dear Lord, as often as I needed You; but I have learned my lesson. You have always been my helper, never forgetting me, never despising me for my forgetfulness. Henceforth I shall live only for You, with You, and in You, all the days of my life. The eternal salvation of my soul is in Your hands; and if I but remember always the ways of Your commandments, Your love, I shall rest secure. Keep me humble, so that I may ever stay close to You."

The Collect follows this same thought: "O God, who has prepared for those who prove their love of You, delights that are hidden from men's eyes, do dispose our hearts with fervent love of You, that we may love You in all things and above all things, and so one day come to enjoy those things that are the reward of love, the treasure of Yourself, which exceeds all the desire of men's hearts." If we could all "be of one mind," as St. Peter counsels in today's Epistle—the mind of God—we should learn how truly the Father loves us.

GRADUAL – Psalm 83:10,9.

In an effort to bring ourselves, first of all, to the desired unanimity of mind, we sing: "O God, be my protector. Look not on my merits, which are nothing, but on the kind face of my Lord and Savior, Jesus Christ, who has given Himself for me. O God of all power, hear my prayer and listen patiently to me."

The humility of the first two words is very forceful. Then the voice reaching up to God asks Him to turn His face down towards us (*aspice Deus*). The same is true in the music of *respice*. God hears, and turns to look on the souls of His lovers (*super servos tuos*). Then, strengthened by that glance of love, we soar to great heights by our confidence in the God of strength (*Deus virtutum*). The *exaudi* is still reaching up to God; but when we recall our place in this vale of tears, the humility of *preces servorum* is very beautiful. In *servorum tuorum* we see a picture of God's servants all over the earth, lifting their hearts to Him in song and drawing His blessings down to earth.

ALLELUIA -- Psalm 20:1.

"My soul, O Lord, will rejoice in Your strength, not its own. In Your salvation, that is, the salvation won for us by Your Son, my soul will rejoice exceedingly."

The music after *Alleluia*, while it continues to use much of that melody, has in it a mixture of joyful song and humble confidence. The latter is especially felt in *Domine in virtute tua*, but *laetibitur rex* takes up the joyful strain. The long series of notes on the simple *et* seems to say: "And besides these treasures and joys, there are still some greater blessings waiting to come down upon (*super*) those who have known the blessing of redemption (*salutare tuum*)." The exceeding rejoicing is evident in *exsultabit vehementer*.

OFFERTORY -- Psalm 15:7,8.

The Gospel reminds us that keeping the commandments is our proof of love. How much God must love us to give us those ten signposts, which lead all who observe them nearer and nearer to Him. The offering of our hearts is accompanied by this very apt song in the Offertory: "O my Lord, I will bless You, for You have put into my heart the desire to know You and Your goodness. I will try to live always in Your presence, for I know You are ever near to help me to be firm in my purpose."

Benedicam Dominum presents the picture of our offertory: hearts and hands raised in love. There is graphic presentation, too, in the music of *tribuit mihi intellectum*. See the firm purpose expressed in the notes of *providebam*—the soul advancing towards

Deum. There is great joy in the singing of *quoniam a dextris*, when we realize that God will always be at our side if we but continue to be on His side. Then the humble realization of whose side He is at, is shown graphically in *mihi ne commovear.*

COMMUNION – Psalm 26:4.

Our offertory, consecrated in the Oblation, has been given back to us in the most precious Gift of heaven. The joy of possessing Him makes us cry out: "One thing I beg very earnestly of You, O Lord: that You will let me dwell near You all my life." The music of the whole Communion is so beautiful that it needs no explanation. The very words seem to sing themselves. In *Domino* and *Domini* a joyful reverence is contained in the music; and the four last words express, as near as it is possible to express in earthly music, the foretaste of eternal happiness that awaits each faithful servant.

SIXTH SUNDAY AFTER PENTECOST

The liturgy of today's Mass and Office is concerned with the two sacraments that are the basis of our Christian life; they are baptism and holy Eucharist. In the Epistle, St. Paul reminds us that we were baptized in Christ's death, but that now He is risen, and we must, because of our baptism, walk in newness of life. Humbly we sing:

INTROIT – Psalm 27:8-9,1.

"You are the strength of my soul and body, O Lord. Under Your protection both shall gain the heaven won for them by You, O Christ. Save me and bless me, for I am Yours, and I come to You. Guide me all my life in the path of perfection, and lift me up, mind and body, that I may always be with You.—I will cry to You, O Lord; do not refuse to answer me, lest I be as one without any hope, whose only end is in the pit of despair."

The approach to God in *Dominus* is very direct, yet the Introit maintains a serious tone throughout. In *fortitudo plebis suae* we hear a simple statement of the truth: that all our strength comes to us because of His sacrifice in our behalf. The music of

Christi sui est tells with reverent thanksgiving what our Lord merited for us. The similarity in the music of *salvum fac populum tuum* and *Dominus* at the beginning, gives greater strength to the parallel ideas contained in both passages. "The Lord is the portion of my inheritance" emphasizes the feeling of the music in *et benedic hereditati tuae*. And the promise on our part, to remember always with how great a price we have been bought, is well sung in *usque in saeculum*.

GRADUAL – Psalm 89:13,1.

"Turn to me, O Lord, and let my prayers prevail upon You to have mercy on me. O Lord, You are ever the refuge and protection of those who serve You." After the sobering thought of the Introit, the soul seems to realize more fully how much need there is of calling for God's help. On *Convertere* the call is a plea rising to God, asking Him to look down upon us.

The music of *Domine* again savors of the great reverence that the composer had for God's Name, for love of which we also pray in today's Collect. The music of *aliquantulum* continues the plea of *Convertere* eloquently, as does *deprecare*. Then *super servos tuos* shows God looking down on us in pity, on all His people all over the world. That one glance of love seems to rouse the soul to the next phase of our song, in the beautiful melody so familiar from other feasts (see especially the Gradual for December 8).

It is very interesting that this gay melody is so aptly sandwiched in between the first melody and the more somber Alleluia music, which follows. It is as though we want to shout from the housetops that God, our refuge, is ever the protector of all who turn in love to Him; we should like the whole world to know the great joy that is to be found in His service. *Factus es nobis* seems to say: "You have lifted us up from death to heaven by our baptism"—us (*nobis*), Your children who, until the saving waters were poured upon our heads, were buried in sin. And You will continue to do that for all men throughout all ages (*progenie*).

ALLELUIA – Psalm 30:2-3.

"My hope is fixed on You, O Lord. Put me not to shame on the last day. You will free me from all my difficulties, if I seek to follow Your most just will. Bend down and listen to me; and in the time of danger to my soul, hurry to my aid." These words and the music for them are of a somber tone.

The reason may be the humble realization that, in spite of our having been lifted to such great heights, we have always to fight the earthly drag downwards of our nature. In *te speravi* we see the soul aspiring to God, but the last notes show the force of nature pulling us down again. That continual warfare between the soul and nature is graphically shown in *non confundar* and *justitia libera me* and *eripe me* and *eripias me*. There is another picture of God inclining to us in the music of *inclina ad me aurem tuam*; and the music of *accelera* lifts us again to Him. So long as we are mindful of the warfare, and strive continually to use all the grace that has come to us, first in baptism and later in very many ways, God will always be on our side to give us at last the privilege of singing an eternal *Alleluia*.

OFFERTORY

This is from Sexagesima Sunday, and is as described for that day.

COMMUNION – Psalm 26:6.

"I will sing to Your Name in thanksgiving, and I will bear willingly the fatigue of the holy Office, that I may sing and praise Your Name in the psalms." The consoling assurance given us in holy Communion moves us to make these words our own as we sing them. The melody is beautiful and ethereal, reaching up into highest heaven, from which God has descended into our souls.

It seems as though God has brought some of heaven with Him. The whole song seems to be our assurance that, having successfully overcome the downward pull of nature, our souls even in this life are privileged to have a foretaste of the great happiness that awaits us. See God's tabernacles towering above the world in *tabernaculo ejus*. See, too, the offering of sacrifice in *hostiam*. Here is another proof that the fullness of the harvest of the holy Sacrifice (the Eucharist) is in proportion to our offering of all that is self: the greater the offering, the greater the harvest; the lower we descend to build up our spiritual life, the higher will be our tower that pierces the sky. So be it—*a generatione et progenie*!

SEVENTH
SUNDAY AFTER PENTECOST

INTROIT – Psalm 46:2.

This is a very happy Sunday in the liturgy of the Mass and the Divine Office. The keynote is, again, the happiness that is to be found in serving God, and it is well expressed in the Introit: "When I stand before You in choir, O my God, let all the earth rejoice with me.—For You are the most high Lord and very much to be reverenced. You are the King of the whole earth."

The reason we are bidden to be joyful could hardly be expressed better than in these words, and the music emphasizes the thought. *Omnes gentes* are all those, of high station and low, who join their hands (*plaudite manibus*) in grateful prayers for the happiness of having been called to God's side. See how the happiness rises in *jubilate*, and note again the reverence of *Deo*. The music that follows is less jubilant on *in voce exsultationis*, because all joy that is of heaven is restrained. The realization that all true joy is to be found only in God, and the highest of this in God's service, reminds us, too, of our complete dependence upon Him.

GRADUAL – Psalm 33:12,6.

"I am Your child by many titles, O Lord. I will listen to You, and You will guide me aright. I will come to You, Lord, and be enlightened; and with the strength of Your grace, I shall not be fearful before You." Our dependence upon God is expressed in these words, also. See the procession of loving children going to the Father in *Venite, filii, audite Me*. God's coming down to earth to teach us the way to Him is pictured in the music of *docebo vos*. Having been taught His gospel of love, still greater numbers follow after him (*Accedite ad eum*).

ALLELUIA – Psalm 46:2.

"When I stand before You in choir, O my God, let all the earth rejoice with me." Here the same picture as above is extended in a very joyful manner. We are bidden to let the joy of our vocation seek its proper level (*jubilate Deo*) and to let our praise be drawn out to its greatest length *in voce exsultationis*.

OFFERTORY – Daniel 3:40.

We renew the sacrifices we made when God first called us to His side. The song we sing today should come from our hearts: "May our sacrifice offered in Your sight today, O Lord, be as acceptable as were the holocausts of rams and goats, and those of thousands of well-fed lambs. And may our offering be every bit as pleasing to You, for there is no embarrassment among those who trust in You, O Lord."

There is a very beautiful melody in the first part of this Offertory, as far as the word *taurorum*. Then at *et sicut* it seems as if a new melody is introduced. Again, at *in conspectu tuo hodie* there is descriptive music that reminds us of the necessity of repeating today the sacrifices we have so often promised. Note the finality of the music in *ut placeat tibi*: God is the only One who is to be satisfied; whatever is His good pleasure must be ours, too. The music on *Domine* might easily have ended on that single note on -*ne*, but the composer could not be satisfied with so little; so he ascends once, repeats the phrase, and finally ends in great reverence.

All sacrifice must be offered to God, for He alone is worthy of all our actions. Yet every sacrifice that we offer to God contributes to our salvation. How little of self should be left in us! We cannot offer our willfulness to God; no sin can stain the hands that hold up the clean Oblation of love. So the complete immolation of self out of pure love of God makes us dwell lovingly on *Domine*. Note the beautiful continuation of this thought in the Secret which follows.

COMMUNION – Psalm 30:3.

"In the fervor of my heart I will cry to You to bend down Your ear and listen to me, O my God, and in the time of danger to hasten to my aid." See the action of God coming down to us in *Inclina*. God has come very close to us in holy Communion; we have been assured that our sacrifice has been consecrated and returned to us in the fullness of God's love.

In today's Epistle we heard: "Now you must make over your natural powers, as slaves to right-doing, till all is sanctified.... you...have become God's slaves, you have a harvest in your sanctification, and your reward is eternal life." However, the Gospel reminds us of our Lord's warning: "The kingdom of heaven will not give entrance to every man who calls me Master, Master, but only to the man who does the will of My Father who is in heaven." May God make haste (*accelera*) to deliver us from all of self that remains, and confirm us in all that is good.

EIGHTH SUNDAY AFTER PENTECOST

INTROIT — Psalm 47:10-11,2.

"You have shown mercy to us, O God, by leaving us Your Presence in the tabernacle. Thus Your Name is held in honor over all the earth, that from every place our praise may go up to You. May the perfection of the religious life be fully given and spread abroad, and more perfectly practiced, through the power and protection of Your right hand.—You are great, O Lord, and most worthy of all the praise I can give to You, in the chapel and on this holy hill where the religious life has been so carefully nurtured by You."

Today's Introit is the same as that sung for our Lady's Purification, February 2. See how beautifully the words fit that feast, as well as today. Both words and music are an inspiring canticle of loving thanksgiving for all the gifts that are ours. We can surely make this Introit a prayer for the millions of souls who do not yet know the joys we have experienced. No doubt, many of them, once they learn of God's love, may surpass us in returning love to Him. What glories the sacraments of baptism and holy Eucharist would hold for them! Our best means of thanking and praising God for having given us such great gifts lies in our making these same graces possible for other souls.

Suscepimus seems to picture us being lifted up to God by the favors we have received from Him. There is reverent joy in the music of *Deus, misericodiam*, and *templi tui*. Then hear the evident joy of *nomen tuum Deus*. There is a meditative stillness in the music that follows *laus tua*, as if the composer were absorbed in the picture of the peace that would come to all the earth, if all men should realize the value of the gift God gives to those who glorify His Name.

The Collect of today's Mass follows fittingly on the glorious Introit: "Grant us, O Lord, the spirit of always thinking of what is right, and doing it, so that we, who cannot live without You, may live always according to Your will." Then we who are heirs, as the Epistle reminds us, have the obligation of using our inheritance wisely and well. Trials and difficulties are often the lot of the heir, but there is no reason for fear as we sing in the Gradual.

GRADUAL – Psalm 30:3; 70:1.

"My good God, You are my Father and protector; my house of refuge, to which I may fly at all times. In You, O Lord, my hope is fixed. Put me not to shame in the last day." Hear the quiet confidence of *Esto mihi* because *in Deum* is our protection. *In locum refugii* gives the picture of a soul flying to God and being assured of safety (*salvum me facias*). Our hearts are lifted to great hope at *Deus, in te speravi,* and the reverence of the composer for the Lord's Name shines forth again in the music of *Domine.* Then confidence and the virtue of hope are glorified in *non confundar in aeternum.*

ALLELUIA – Psalm 47:2.

"Great is the Lord, and exceedingly to be praised, in the city of our God, in His holy mountain." This verse brings us the picture of how God is praised in the courts of heaven. We of earth cannot yet be perfect in our praise. But we are bidden to imitate here, in our chapels, as closely as we can, that song of praise sung by angels and saints, in order that we may thus prepare ourselves more fittingly to add our voices one day to the eternal *Alleluia.* This thought, instead of giving cause for pride, reminds us of how really little we are able to do of ourselves.

OFFERTORY – Psalm 17:28,32.

Only God's graces, through the gifts He sends us, enable us to see the value of offering all of self to Him, each time we are present at the holy Sacrifice. So, as we offer our gift today, we sing: "If I stay humble, You will save me, O my God; but if I am proud, You will humiliate me. There is none like to You, O God. Whom can I trust as I can trust You?"

The music of *Populum tuum humilem* shows the humble offering of God's people, who are lifted in safety (*salvum facies*) from the attachments of the world to God (*Domine*). Then *et oculos* expresses the idea of our sacrifice reaching God's attention; yet that of the proud man (*superborum*) does not belong to God, but descends to earth. Only the humble (*humiliabis*) are lifted up to Him. "He hath cast down the mighty from their seats, and hath exalted the humble." The final music is the exaltation that fills the soul when we realize how truly privileged we are in our vocation.

COMMUNION – Psalm 33:9.

"O my Lord, let me taste how sweet You are; and bless me, for I do trust in You." The greatest of all graces, the Source of every grace, comes to us in holy Communion, and our souls are filled with sweet grace as we sing these words. Then we, who find grace, peace, and happiness in the sacrament of Love, cannot be satisfied with hugging this great privilege to ourselves; we must, from that very grace, do all in our power to help other people partake of this same great joy.

The music of *Gustate et videte* is a glad cry to all peoples to sample the joy of serving God in love. It is not an impassioned shout of joy, but one of zealous pleading. The *quoniam* shows God descending from heaven into our hearts with *omne delectamentum*; and the reverence of *Dominus* seems to say, "*O quam suavis est.*" Finally the music of *beatus vir* expresses the true happiness of soul that God gives those who love him. How zealous today's liturgy should make us to share our life of grace with other souls!

NINTH SUNDAY AFTER PENTECOST

The theme of today's liturgy is to be found in the Epistle: "He who thinks he stands firmly should beware of a fall." All our trust must be placed in the grace that comes from living the Christ-life, of seeking only to do God's will. This is expressed clearly for us in the prayer of the Introit.

INTROIT – Psalm 53:6-7.

"I trust in You, O my God, and look to You for assistance, for You are the protector of my soul. Keep far from me all these forces that would hurt my soul, and let their lying words no longer disturb me.—Save me, O God, for I call upon Your holy Name. I submit myself to Your judgment, for I know it is tempered by Your love for me; I shall stand for You always; do You stand by me." This is a peaceful, confident song from a heart grounded in humility. The music of the first four words seems to say, very humbly, "Just see how good God is, to stoop down to me and help me!" That which follows portrays God lifting our souls up to Him; and *averte...Domine* has the action of God's intervening grace, coming down to scatter the enemies of our souls and keep our hearts directed to Him.

GRADUAL – Psalm 8:2.

The Collect expresses the desire of true followers of Christ: that is, those things that are according to God's will. The realization that God will hear our prayer seems to be the motive for our singing in a spirit of confidence in the Gradual: "My God, how great and glorious You are in the whole earth. Would that I could fully understand and appreciate Your glory!"

The reverence of *Domine, Dominus noster* is very prayerful. Then see how it rises in great joy at *admirabile*, and then reverently again comes *nomen tuum*. The expanse of *universa terra* is well shown in the music. And how graphic is the music of *elevata est*: God's benefits literally rain down upon us in *super caelos*.

ALLELUIA – Psalm 58:2.

"O my God, deliver my soul from the power of evil spirits, and help me to overcome those evil impulses that arise within me." This is a quiet song, but very beautiful. The *Eripe* seems to lift us up from the things of earth to God; the pleading of *Deus meus* is made especially beautiful by the similar phrasing of the notes on both words. Note the humility expressed in placing the music of *Deus* higher than that of *meus*, as if the saintly composer would have us ever mindful of our own position, depending entirely on God. In *et ab insurgentibus* we find the same feeling as in *Eripe* above. The *libera me*, while it is sung to the Alleluia music, is also symbolic of our clinging to God and depending on Him to lift us up constantly from evil impulses.

OFFERTORY

This was considered for the third Sunday of Lent. It fits beautifully into today's schema, also.

COMMUNION – John 6:57.

"He who eats My Flesh, and drinks My Blood, lives continually in Me, and I live in him, says the Lord." The reward of living humbly, dependent upon God, is God Himself. So our souls sing out His own words. Note the strength of *manducat*, especially the accented syllable. It emphasizes what Monsignor Hellriegel speaks of in his *Holy Sacrifice of the Mass*: *"he who eats."* We can almost hear our Lord saying these words in the simple melody with which they are clothed.

The rise at *sanguinem* reminds us that His Blood flowed freely for our salvation when He was "lifted up" on the Cross. Then *in me manet* gives us the hope of being lifted up with our Lord. Again the gentle voice of Christ seems to promise—*et ego in eo*—that He will always come down to those humble souls who put all their trust in Him. The last two words seem entirely out of the setting of the music that has preceded. But that is as it should be, and it serves the better to make our Lord's words ever so much more forceful. May we learn from today's liturgy the lesson taught therein—humbly to place ourselves in the way of God's will, so that we may taste here the joy of having God dwell in us, and thus ensure for ourselves the happiness of dwelling with Him throughout eternity.

TENTH SUNDAY AFTER PENTECOST

Knowing not what lies before us in our journey to God, we "do not ask to see," but placing all our trust in Him, we face the future. That seems to be the underlying theme in the Mass and Office today. The Gospel, telling of the proud man and the humble penitent, begins with the words: "Some, who had confidence in themselves, thought they had won acceptance with God." If, doubting our own ability to advance unaided in virtue, we have looked to God, then may we most truthfully sing:

INTROIT — Psalm 54:17,18,20,23,2.

"When I have cried to You, O my God, I could be sure that You would save me. There are many who would try to disturb me if they did not realize that You will humble them. But I will put all my trust in You, my Lord, and You will support and nourish my soul." "Hear me, O God, when I cry to You, and turn not away from my petition; graciously attend to me and hear me."

Our cry in *dum clamarem* rises perceptibly *ad Dominum*, and there's happiness in *vocem meam*, because God has so favorably heard us. The music of *approprinquant mihi* seems to say, "God has looked down from heaven on me, and because He saw that I trusted not myself, 'He has regarded the humility' of His servant, and has lifted me up over my enemies (*humiliavit eos*)." From all eternity God, who dwells in eternity, has extolled those who place their trust in Him, bringing them to the greatest heights of glory; this is the force of the music at *qui est...in aeternum*. In the last words of the Introit there seems to be a picture of manna falling from heaven—*ipse te enutriet*: "God will nourish our souls with Himself." *Panis angelicus fit panis hominum.*

GRADUAL — Psalm 16:8,2.

Thought of God's care of us leads us very humbly to sing in the Gradual: "Keep me as the apple of Your eye, quite close to You, O Lord, that I may never resist Your will. Guard me from all danger, as if under the shadow of Your wings. I will trust Your judgment, for I know You will be kind to me for the sake of Your Son in whom I trust.

114

The plea for God to keep us (*custodi me*) is very direct and simple, and only expands reverently on that word so sacred to the composer, *Domine*. Perhaps my imagination is overdeveloped, but the music of *pupillam* assumes something of the form of that part of the eye, while the two last groups of notes on *occuli* more surely picture the two eyes. Note the shade trees that are pictured by the notes at *umbra alarum tuarum*, and the all-encircling protection of *protege me*. At *De vultu tuo* we lift our eyes to God's face in a familiar melody, only to find that His eyes (*oculi tui videant*) look without partiality on all men, all over the world. What peace comes into the soul when we are able to see all men with God's eyes! Then we can more joyfully sing our Alleluia.

ALLELUIA – Psalm 64:2.

"I have been chosen by You, my God, to render You that praise which all should give to You. By my vows I have devoted myself to Your service." "It is fitting to raise a hymn," says the music of *Te decet* in a graphic manner, but almost immediately the word *Deus* becomes very holy. *In Sion* tells us that *Sion* is heaven and those places on earth where God's glory is hymned. *Et tibi*...lifts our praise to the heights. Yet, notice how clearly it brings out the truth of the fact that an offering of our vows to God exalts us to great heights, while at the same time it brings showers of blessings down from heaven upon us.

This same thought is continued in the beautiful Offertory, which we sang on the first Sunday of Advent, and now chant again today. The thoughts that filled our hearts on that Sunday are in a special manner applicable to today's Offertory.

COMMUNION – Psalm 50:21.

Having tasted the harvest of the Sacrifice, we sing gladly: "Dear Lord, let me give You freely whatever sacrifice You so justly ask of me for the rest of my life. Nothing that I can give can ever repay You for Your infinite goodness to me." One can almost see hands lifted up in offering at *acceptabis*. It is a just sacrifice, surely a *sacrificium justitiae* which God asks us to lift up to Him. Notice how the group of three notes on the last syllable of *oblationes* is repeated at *per* and *tuum*. It is a triple offering, and carries the melody along in three *sursum corda*'s, lifting our hearts with it. Then the final word is one that should be sung with the tenderest love. It is full of reverence, thanksgiving, and adoration. The soul that realizes the value of having given all its confiding trust to God has received a foretaste of heaven as a reward. Only the loftiest sentiments can fill our souls as we realize how privileged we are to have so intimate a place at the altar of sacrifice. It is the pledge of our *Dominum qui est ante saecula, et manet in aeternum.*

ELEVENTH SUNDAY AFTER PENTECOST

INTROIT — Psalm 67:6-7,36,2.

"You are our God, dwelling in our midst (in the holy tabernacle). You have deigned to allow us to live in Your holy company; the power You will give to us is that of holiness.—Arise, O God, in Your might, and put Your enemies to flight; make them that hate You fly in fear from before Your face."

The music on the word *Deus* sounds like surprise, but it is followed by reverent awe in the next three words, that God would dwell with us, the same God who dwells in heaven and in His Church! Then when that particular melody seems to come to an end, we find a new strain. Notice how the notes for *Deus, qui habitare* are all between the first and second lines of the staff, indicating how close we are together when we are with God. The music for *unanimes in domo* seems to lift our eyes to heaven, where we shall be one in God's home. And then for a third time the music seems to change. It takes on a brave note, because we recognize that when we are one with God, His strength is our strength; and the final notes on *suae* bring us back to the first feeling of awe, ending with the same music as on *suo.*

GRADUAL — Psalm 27:7,1.

"Give me a trustful heart, O God, and in Your mercy let me win Your protection and help. My body shall rejoice in Your help. Now that my will is given to You, I will praise You with all my being. I will cry to You, O Lord; do not refuse to answer me, lest I be as one without any help."

These words are the Psalmist's, but we could (and should) make them our own. However, when we recall the words of the Epistle that just preceded them, we should think of these as the words of the risen Christ. See how the music, too, seems to suggest this: the calmness, the dignity, and the simplicity of such a beautiful phrase as *refloruit caro mea*. On *voluntate* and *confitebor* the soul reaches up to God, ending lovingly on *illi*. Then, too, notice how the voice of Christ, crying to the Father (*clamavi*), pierces the heavens. There is almost a plaintiveness in the music of *Deus meus* before the *ne sileas* again reaches up to God as a final cry, and *ne discedas* ends in a humble trust in the Father's help. We may sing this as Christ, risen and glorified, would sing it, but we must make it our own, too, since we who seek the things that are above profess to be risen with Him.

ALLELUIA – Psalm 80:2-3.

"I will rejoice before You, O my God, my only helper. I will sing unto You for You are my God. I will sing a psalm to You as the organ, too, peals forth the same joy."

The possibility of singing with Christ to the Father fills us with a joy that only *Alleluia* can express. Note, however, the restraint in that joy on *Exsultate...Jacob*. Only on *psalmum jucundum* does it rise to any height, returning finally to the restrained ending, recalling to our minds so many of the counsels of spiritual perfection presented in the seminary and novitiate.

OFFERTORY – Psalm 29:2-3.

"I will praise You, O Lord, for all Your kindness to me, taking me in Your hand and not letting evil spirits rejoice in my fall. I have cried to You so often, and You have forgiven me and helped me, O my God."

The fact that this Offertory is repeated from Ash Wednesday's Mass is interesting. For that day, the words may seem not to have been in keeping with the spirit of Lent, but when we realize that at the conclusion of Lent comes the resurrection, then this offertory seems quite apropos.

In the Gospel just sung, we can imagine the man whose speech was restored singing these words to God in humble thanksgiving. The *Ephpheta* reminds us, also, of the time the same word was uttered over us in baptism. The music is very simple, like that of a child learning to speak. Notice especially the notes on *nec de-lec-tasti.* Then, as confidence comes, the *clamavi* goes up to God and ends gratefully and humbly on *sanasti me.*

Since our ears were opened in baptism, how many times have we heard God's words, how many times have we heard His voice speaking to us! Notice in the Gospel that Jesus took the deaf man "aside from the crowd." So, too, do we hear and understand better when we are "aside from the crowd," listening alone to God's words. Then, also, are we better able to preach the Gospel by word and by example.

COMMUNION – Proverbs 3:9-10.

"Give honor to the Lord with what you have, and with the first of your fruits; then your barns will be filled with abundance, and your wine presses will run over with wine." There are two commands in the first part of this song, and then two promises. It is God the Father speaking to us, telling us that if we are mindful of Him, He will reward beyond measure our offerings of sacrifice. In our offertory we gave ourselves, and now in holy Communion God gives us back our gifts, consecrated—Himself entirely. The music also seems to accentuate the four divisions: the simplicity of *honora Dominum* is followed by the heights to which we may reach with our gifts; but then God goes still higher (*impleantur horrem*), piling up His gifts for us. The limpid flow of the last phrase seems to portray the wine running through the presses.

Perhaps we can best sum up today's liturgy (both words and music) in this thought: we should continually praise God for the benefits that have come to us since our baptism. We have risen with Christ to a life of generosity in His service. God's arm is not shortened rewarding us.

TWELFTH
SUNDAY AFTER PENTECOST

There is one picture in all the various parts of the liturgy today: each one of us is in danger of falling into the hands of wicked men, but we are continually saved from such a fate only because God is constantly solicitous of our eternal welfare. When we do succumb, our wounds are healed and bound up; we are strengthened by the oil and wine of sacramental grace. Of our-ourselves we would be unable to arise; hence, like the man who fell victim to the robbers, we cry plaintively in the
INTROIT – Psalm 69:2-3,4.

"O God, You are my only helper and sure protector. Hurry and help me. In Your kindness, take from the evil spirits their power to hurt me. Drive them back to their prison, for they cease not to plot against me."

In the music, the man lying on the ground seems to have difficulty in calling upon God, but once he begins, his cries go up. There is anguish in *Domine*, and then a hurried insistence on *ad adjuvandum me festina*, followed almost by a vindictiveness in *confundantur et revereantur inimici mei*. The injured man, however, seems to realize that it is only God who can rid him of his enemies. This Introit might also be considered as the cry of Christ in the Garden of Gethsemane.

In the Epistle, St. Paul puts these words into our mouths: "We are not able to do anything for ourselves; our sufficiency comes from God."
GRADUAL – Psalm 33:1-2.

"I bless You, O my God, for allowing me to spend my time in singing Your praises all day. Make me, O Lord, meek and humble of heart, and my soul shall rejoice in Your glory."

The *benedicam* is humble, reminding us how we should feel about our privilege of singing God's praises. The *Dominum* lifts us up to God, and the music of *omni tempore* suggests the length of days to be spent with God in heaven. *Semper laus ejus* shows us the angels bowing in adoration before God, bidding us, too, to remember that *ore meo* must continue to sing the delights of heaven. *In Domine* shows our hearts reaching up to God and His gifts coming down to us, to continually lift us up to Him. Then the *audient* is very humble, but *mansueti* gives us proof that those who practice humility will continually be lifted up; and so it is that our joy (*laetentur*) is of heaven, the highest. Notice how the music of *Dominum* in the first line is repeated in *Domino* in the fifth: when we lift our voices to bless God, the same God blesses us. He will not be outdone in generosity.

ALLELUIA — Psalm 87:2.

"O Lord, my God, who has purchased salvation for me, to You do I cry both in the day and during the night." If we recall again the picture of the man spoken of in the Gospel, lying helpless upon the earth and calling to God for help, we shall have a better understanding of how *Domine Deus* is to be sung: with reverent confidence, because *salutis meae* is a heavenly gift. *In die* we can lift our voices high to God, but as night comes we are restrained. It is fitting, then, that *coram te* repeats the music of *Alleluia*. Recall once more that *Alleluia* has been interpreted as "a song of praise for Him who is."

OFFERTORY — Exodus 32:11,13,14.

At the end of the story of the Good Samaritan, the lawyer answer's Christ's question, "Which of these three proved himself neighbor? And he said, 'He who took pity on him.' " The words of the Offertory, an unusually long one, seem to give us another example of mercy—that shown by God.

"Moses prayed in the sight of the Lord, his God, and said: 'Why, O Lord, is Your indignation roused against Your people? Let the anger of Your mind cease; remember Abraham, Isaac, and Jacob, to whom You promised to give a land flowing with milk and honey.' And the Lord was appeased from doing the evil which He had spoke of doing." The prayer of Moses, the evidence he produces of God's promise to the three patriarchs, is followed by the answer: God's mercy will be granted.

In the music there is duplication of the introduction. I could not find the reason for this, but it seemed to me that one of the early transcribers of the music made a mistake in copying when he came to the end of *sui*; someone brought this to his attention, and he re-wrote it, perhaps intending to delete the first transcription. The repetition can scarcely be attributed to emphasis, since the introduction does not need it. Had *memento...mel* been repeated for emphasis, it would be understandable. However, both renditions give the same picture of Moses, standing with his hands joined, humbly preparing himself to speak to God (a good picture of the recollection necessary before prayer).

The first *et dixit* reaches a little higher towards God. It is a little bolder, perhaps; but here, too, may be the answer to the duplication. On second thought, Moses may have felt that it would be more fitting if he were a little more lowly. The *quare* is a querulous searching, but the condescension in *Domine* is almost apologetic. *Irasceris* is shouted because Moses is distressed about the plight of *populo tuo* being brought so low. Then in *Parce* and *memento* he seems to become excited and the three patriarchs' names are treated as belonging to those who are among the highest of God's friends. The strain then seems to subside in *dare terram, fluentem lac,* and calmly ends with *et mel.* In the last part there seems to be a picture of God's mercy (*et placatus*): God is ever faithful to His promises.

To anyone merely glancing through the principal parts of the Mass, it might seem that there is no connection; it skips from one thing to another. As we study the parts we sing in each Mass, however, we can see the oneness of the liturgy in each instance. The whole picture is made up, like a precious mosaic, of many parts, each of which has its place in completing the scene and the lesson that the Church would hold before our eyes.

COMMUNION – Psalm 103:13,14-15.

"The whole earth, O Lord, is filled with fruits from Your kind hands; You bring bread from the earth and wine to cheer the heart of man; to make the face of man cheerful with oil, and strengthen his heart with bread."

While these words have a direct connection with the events recorded in the Gospel, their practical application carries on the idea expressed in the Offertory, and here refer especially to the Bread and Wine which have just strengthened our hearts in holy Communion.

The melody is a beautiful, simple song that makes us think of the people in the fields at this time of the year, singing simply and joyfully as they go about their tasks. The ascending notes on *terram* and *vinum* seem to indicate growth coming up out of the earth. *Laetificet* and *exhilaret* are joyous, but *in oleo* is as quiet as healing should be. In the final phrase our heart (*cor hominis*) is lifted up by "the pledge of future glory which is given to us."

A fitting recessional in keeping with the beauty of today's liturgy can be found in the Gradual: Bless the Lord always; let His praise be ever on our lips!

THIRTEENTH SUNDAY AFTER PENTECOST

INTROIT – Psalm 73:20,19,23,1.

"Remember, O Lord, You promised that You would never forget the poor who are in trouble. Arise, God, judge Your own cause, and do not close Your ears to the voices of those who call to You.—Why, O divine Shepherd, does it appear as if You cast us away from You? Is Your anger kindled against us who are sheep of Your flock?"

The music of the first two words, *Respice, Domini!*—again, the clarion call—is the voice of the ten lepers crying from the distance. Even the music of those two words seems to indicate that it is a cry from anxious hearts. *In testamentum tuum* we find stressed the promise that our heavenly Father sent from above. Then there is a very pathetic strain in *et animas...finem*, which is touching in its appeal. The desperate men raise their voices higher still, lest they be not heard: *exsurge Domine!* The music for *et judica causam tuam* should be sung a little faster—the lepers, trying to find something to touch the Heart of Christ, go on breathlessly in the same strain through *et ne obliviscar* to the end.

GRADUAL – Psalm 73:20,19,22.

The words of the Gradual are practically the same as those of the Introit; the last verse is different: "Remember the reproaches which the foolish sinner casts upon You."

Here in the Gradual the music is quite different from the importunate cry heard in the Introit; now it is the voice of Mother Church reminding the eternal Father of His promise to sinners.

Now *Respice Domine* is the plaintive cry of a loving mother for her erring children. There is a note of sadness in the phrase *et animas pauperum tuorum*; and the plea to remember His promise (*ne obliviscaris in finem*) seems to pierce the heavens. *Exsurge* shows God arising in judgment; *judica causam tuam* pictures the judgment as coming from heaven, and therefore, it is a just judgment. "Do thou, in heaven, recall (*memor esto*), O Lord, how punishment (*opprobrium*) was sent down from heaven on Your lowly *servorum* who, though of earth, nevertheless belonged to You (*tuorum*).

ALLELUIA − Psalm 89:1.

"O Lord, You are always the refuge of those who serve You." The Alleluia is a simple but joyful melody, as if the understanding Mother is confident that God will answer her prayer. The Lord (*Domine*) who went up to heaven from earth now stoops down to protect us (*refugium*), lifting us (*nobis*) up with Him. In the music there seems to be the indication that He will always do His part, to the end of time, to bring sinners back to Him, if they will but turn from the leprosy of sin.

OFFERTORY − Psalm 30:15,16.

Each one of the ten lepers and holy Mother Church seem to sing: "I will put my trust in You, O Lord; I have acknowledged You as my God. My whole life is in Your hands."

The music of *In te speravi* pictures the lifting of hands and hearts from earth to *Domine*, who bows down to hear our prayer. There is some boasting in *dixi*, but it is an honest expression of the fidelity with which has been taught the dominion of *Deus meus*. From *in manibus* to *mea* are to be seen again the gifts of God's hands coming down to us. We can also see here the absolution which comes to us in the sacrament of penance, wiping out our leprosy.

COMMUNION − Wisdom 16:20.

The soul, refreshed by sacramental grace, is ready to receive Bread from heaven, which is given by God. "It has in it all that is delicious, and the sweetness of every taste."

The Communion is a fine Eucharistic hymn that could be sung as a motet for Benediction or at other times. There is beautiful reverence in the music of the first three words, rising with the motions of the soul on *nobis Domine*. The simplicity of the melody is elaborated only on *delectamentum, saporem*, and *suavitatis*, emphasizing the joy of soul of those who are free from the leprosy of sin, and who, partaking of God's Food, are joined to Him and to all other members of the Mystical Body of Christ. "I am the Vine, you are the branches; unless you abide in Me, you cannot have life in you."

FOURTEENTH
SUNDAY AFTER PENTECOST

The motif of today's liturgy is to be found in the Communion (from the Gospel), *Quaerite primum regnum Dei*. Our human weakness is ever ready to make us fall, says the Collect, and the Epistle from St. Paul reminds us of the continual struggle between the "spirit and the flesh" that the Gospel calls, "God and mammon." We are Christ-ians; so we must establish the kingdom of Christ in our hearts first of all (*Primum*) before we can be instrumental in bringing it to others. By our vocation, we have no other choice: Christ has asked us to come, follow Him, and when we took up the Cross to do so, we signified our intention of being always on God's side. In the

INTROIT – Psalm 83:10,11,2-3.

we sing: "O God, be my protector. Look not on my merits, which are nothing, but on the kind face of my Lord and Savior, Jesus Christ, who has given Himself for me. Let me love the life to which You have called me, and let me prefer it to all the liberty I could have in the world without You.—O my Lord, I will strive to appreciate the beauty of the life to which you have called me. Your home, indeed, is full of delight and beauty. Let me learn from the life in the cloister (convent, seminary) to long for Your house, of which this is only the court."

The music of *protector noster* is a confident melody, full of joyous faith. Notice that the lowest note on pro-*te*-ctor is the beginning of a rising group (see also *faciem* and *super*) which leads to greater heights. The *aspice* and *respice* are not so sharp as, for example, the *Respice* of last Sunday's Introit, but they do command attention.

GRADUAL – Psalm 117:8,9.

Following the advice given in the Epistle, we sing: "I will be careful not to put my trust in anyone but You, my Lord. I cannot rely on myself, but I will throw myself with confidence on You and not on man. I will let my hope not rest on anyone save You, my God. No matter how holy another may seem to me, all that is of worth in his sanctity is from You, and I shall be safer if I put my trust in You."

The first phrase, *Bonum est*, reminds us of the confidence found in the first words of the Introit (compare it with the Gradual of the fourth Sunday after Pentecost). *Confidere* pictures us reaching up to God (*in Domino*) who mercifully bends down His ear to hear our prayer. The music of *confidere in homine* reminds us of those people who are continually running about telling their troubles to others; they go far and wide, and yet no solution to their problem seems to be found. The next *bonum est* is very joyful, but note the simplicity of *sperare*: it is calm, settled, because it is hope *in Domino*. On the contrary, the *sperare in principibus* is about the same as *confidere in homine* above.

ALLELUIA – Psalm 94:1.

This is a simple melody, but like the Introit and the Gradual it is the simplicity of joyful confidence. Notice how *venite* and *salutari* seem like introductions, or "leads" to the words which follow. In the spirit of today's liturgy, it is fitting that we who have been dedicated to the work of the spirit, should sing this invitation for others to "come and see" the delights which God has reserved for His faithful sons and daughters.

OFFERTORY – Psalm 33:8,9.

"To those who fear You with a loving fear, O Lord, You will send Your angels to be constantly about them to protect them. O my Lord, give me to taste how sweet You are." Here is another melody full of confidence. Note the resemblance between *quia melior*... of the Introit, and *gustate*... of this hymn. Just to look at the music gives us the picture of angels hovering about, being sent to surround us with their protection. The music of

Dominus is particularly beautiful, emphasizing the idea of which we have been singing.

COMMUNION – Matthew 6:33.

Perhaps I should have said in the beginning that all of today's music seems to be inspired with joyful confidence, for here again (Seek ye first the kingdom of God) we have another fine example. The music of *regnum Dei* is simple, but the very simplicity makes it beautiful. If the two last words of the Communion are sung very softly, it will bring out much better the counsel contained in the words which precede.

In this connection it will be interesting to note the words and music of the Magnificat antiphon which follow. Why were the words of the Communion *Primum quaerite* and not *Quaerite primum*, as in the antiphon? In each case the notes for *quaerite* seem to indicate a searching, and *primum* is like the index finger raised: First! The Vesper antiphon is a spirited piece of music; it could well be used as one of the sung ejaculations at night prayers, or on certain feasts at benediction. The last two notes of the *alleluia* which occurs today could be the final notes for *vobis*, instead of the present *mi, fah*.

FIFTEENTH SUNDAY AFTER PENTECOST

This Sunday's theme may be said to be that of the beatitude: "Blessed are the merciful, for they shall obtain mercy."

INTROIT – Psalm 85:1-3.

This is a beautiful hymn asking God to look with pity on us: "Bend down Your ear to me, O Lord, for I am in great want of Your help. Make me safe. I long to serve You faithfully, and I put my whole trust in You. Have mercy on me, O Lord, for in my weakness I have looked to You for help. Give joy to my soul, O Lord, for I have lifted up my heart to You."

There are three divisions in the music, each of which begins with an imperative command: *inclina, salvum fac,* and *miserere*. Yet, only the first seems peremptory in its clarion call; it is not demanding, but is rather a cry for mercy, reaching up to *Domine*, who does incline His ear *et exaudi me*. There is deep humility and reverence in the music of *salvum fac servum tuum*, particularly in the rendition of *Deus*, while the *meus* which follows seems to lift us up because of our hope.

The next phrase, *miserere mihi*, should be sung with conviction; the *Domine* which follows expresses our humility in so crying to God. The *quoniam* descends unusually low, because I am so helpless without Your mercy. I am so unable of myself to rouse myself to acts of mercy towards others; that is why I must cry to You, O Lord, throughout the entire *tota die*. It is not out of place here for the psalm verse to be one of great joy: that joy comes from having been lifted out of the depths by the mercy of God. Hence, the Collect asks: "Let Your pity continue, O Lord, to cleanse and protect Your Church."

In the Epistle St. Paul points out to the Galatians (and, of course, to us) the duty of instructing others in a spirit of meekness, of bearing one another's burdens, of not growing tired in doing good "to all men." We who have benefited by God's infinite mercy must be merciful to all.

GRADUAL – Psalm 91:2-3.

The thought of the Epistle is continued here. "It is good for me to give all the praise I can to You, my Lord, and to sing to Your holy Name in the Divine Office, for You are the most high God. The burden of my song shall be of Your mercy to me, giving me a new day wherein to praise You, and meditate on Your fidelity to me in the quiet of the night." A grateful person saying "How good you are," comes to our mind when we hear the music of *bonum est*—how good it is! Then immediately the soul seems to rise to *Domino*, blessing His *Altissime* Name.

In the next phrase, the morning song starts out simply enough, but caught on wings it scales the heights, like the sun climbing the heavens. In singing of God's mercy and His truth, we want all to hear our song; all over the world we would send it, until the "night begins to lower."

ALLELUIA – Psalm 94:3.

"For You alone are the great God, O Lord, and a great King above all who act as if they had divine power." Our *Alleluia* is because God is so great (*magnus*), great in His mercy, in His truth, and all His attributes. The expression *magnus* in both instances repeats the music almost identically, coupling in our minds "mercy and truth," "God and King."

We need hardly make any remark concerning the music of *super omnem terram*; just to look at the notes gives us the picture of God's dominion over all the nations of the earth. It would be good to make this hymn a prayer today, that God's mercy may become known to all nations, and at the same time, that all men may recognize His truth. Then surely His mercy will follow.

The Gospel today is a beautiful story of God's mercy. The widow of Naim must have told many times to her relatives and her neighbors of the tender mercy of Jesus. I have often wondered what part the young man took after he arose from the dead. Did he follow Christ? How? Between his first and final death, did he build up grace in his soul? In baptism we were raised from the death of soul to life by the same divine, merciful Jesus. And we? Have we responded to God's grace?

OFFERTORY – Psalm 39:2,3,4.

Blessed, indeed, are we, if we can sing of our interim the words of the Offertory: "O Lord, I constantly look to You and put my trust in You; You are so good to listen to me. In past difficulties You have heard my prayer, and have mercifully brought me out of sin and shame by allowing me time to repent. You have allowed me to sing to You in the choir, and to hymn Your praise with the angels."

What a privilege is ours to sing the mercies of the Lord with the widow of Naim, and with all those who obtained material benefits from Christ's passing so close to them! See how the soul is lifted up in the first two words of the Offertory, and then the humble admission that it has all been due to *Dominum*. The *respexit* is the open, clear look of God into the soul; and again in *exaudivit* we have the picture of God bending down to listen to our cry for mercy. The notes of *in os meum* seem to be a picture; *canticum novum* reminds us that our song is from heaven, and *hymnum Deo nostro* should tell us once more of the mercies that have been handed down to us, which we, in turn, must hand down to others.

COMMUNION – John 6:52.

"...they shall obtain mercy." The Communion, from the Gospel according to St. John, has us sing of that great mercy daily shown to us in holy Communion. "The Bread that I will give you is My flesh for the life of the world." The words make us realize again the part we have in the Mystical Body: we are not alone, receiving His Flesh; we are but stewards, we might say, who must use and share our gift to help others enjoy life in Christ. "The life of the world"—and yet, so much of the world seems to be dead; so many seem to refuse to recognize Him who is their Life. When our Lord first said those words to His apostles, He must have thrilled them with the message He gave them. We must try to sing those words in that same spirit.

In *panis* we see that our Lord is lifting up material bread and consecrating it. Notice *ego*—I, the God of heaven—and *dedero*—hand down from heaven to you. *Caro mea est*—it is My flesh which was born of man for you, and I came down from heaven to inhabit that flesh. *Pro saeculi vita* reminds us of His other words: "Unless you eat the flesh of the Son of man...you cannot have life in you." And we know that the "life" in us is not of earth, but *futurae gloriae nobis pignus datur*. Again, we have in this Communion song a fine motet for a holy hour or benediction.

SIXTEENTH SUNDAY AFTER PENTECOST

"Blessed are the meek." Our Lord implies that meekness and humility are similar virtues ("Learn of Me, for I am meek and humble of heart"). Today's liturgy teaches the value of humility in the Christian life: it begins with the humble cry of the Introit, the Collect, the humble admission of St. Paul to the Ephesians, the beautiful Gospel story ending with the words, "For everyone who exalts himself shall be humbled...," and all through the remaining parts of the Proper.

INTROIT – Psalm 85:3,5.

"Have mercy on me, O Lord, for I have cried to You for help, because You are sweet and mild and have an infinite store of mercy for all who call upon You.—Bend down Your ear to me, O Lord, for I am in great need of Your help."

The music for the first three words seems to say: Look down on my lowliness, O most High. *Quoniam* continues the thought of God bending down to our cry, which goes on, and up to Him, *tota die*. So far the music has been almost a *De profundis*, but now, confident of God's ever-abiding help, the soul soars first on *Domine*, pausing only to express calmly *mitis es*, before singing happily the fullness (*copiosus*) of God's mercy to all (*omnibus*) who lift their voice to God, who in His charity hands down His heavenly gifts to all *invocantibus te*. (See also the Introit for the third Sunday after Pentecost for a similar explanation.) The

GRADUAL

of today's Proper is the same as that for the third Sunday after Epiphany. See the explanation on page 28. In his Letter, St. Paul tells us that if we are rooted and grounded in love, we shall be filled with the fullness of God, "who is able to accomplish all things in a measure far above what we ask or conceive."

ALLELUIA – Psalm 97:1.

Conscious of the above truth, we sing: "O my God, I will sing a new song to You every day, for You are ever most wonderful in Your patience with me."

How truly are we lifted up in *cantate Dominum canticum* with a joy that savors of heaven. Our new song is one which we ourselves have composed, and consequently it is a little less than that of the angels (*novum*). The final words again picture to us the wonderful favors that God so generously lavishes on us while we are still in this vale of tears.

OFFERTORY – Psalm 39:14,15.

"O Lord, look upon me and help me; take from the evil spirits their power to hurt me; O Lord, look upon me." This must be our own heartfelt prayer to God, but we can also think of how it might have been the prayer of the sick man who had been healed, as if he were saying: "O good Master, please help me; these Pharisees who pretend holiness are proud men who have been able to do nothing for me, but do Thou, Good Shepherd, help me. I believe You can do so."

The repetition of the opening words at the close (and the music is repeated, too) makes the prayer a confident one, full of loving faith. It is a simple, unexcited hymn, stating the case with humility and faith. The music seems to imply: "Look down upon me, Lord, and see the condition I am in." Sing the first line a little slowly, with this thought in mind. Then *confundantur et revereantur* express the anguish of a soul tortured by evil, who knows that only God can *auferant eam*. See how easily the *fah, fah, doh* at the end of *eam* lead the singer back to the first melody; this time that melody should be sung with insistence and confidence that God will hear our prayer.

COMMUNION – Psalm 70:16-17,18.

"I will always remember, O Lord, your eternal justice, which urges you to have mercy on me because I am so weak. You have been my teacher from my youth, allowing me to be brought up in the faith of your holy Church. In my old age forsake me not, but keep me under Your protection, even till my hair is greyed." This hymn, unlike the Blessed Sacrament motets we have had on the past few Sundays, is rather a humble admission of how greatly we have been dependent on God for all we receive from Him.

The music of *Domine* is the reverent approach to God of a soul trying to express its thanks after receiving Him in holy Communion. *Solius* shows how God alone has been our helper. Then the next phrases seem to portray the soul of the grateful communicant when he realizes that God has been with him from babyhood, through his joyful youth (*iuventute*) and even in the loneliness (*senectam et senium*) of old age. The repetition of the three notes on *ne derelinquas me* are joyful because the humble soul knows that God will continue ever to lift him up through His presence, until the final lifting up to heaven.

SEVENTEENTH
SUNDAY AFTER PENTECOST

As we come towards the end of the liturgical year, it will be noticed that the Proper of the Mass and Office contains more and more references to the general judgment. Today we are reminded that if we walk in the way of love we need have no fear of the judgment. As St. John says in his Letter, "Love wipes out fear; the man who fears has not yet learned to love."

INTROIT — Psalm 118:137,124; 1.

"You are just, O Lord, and Your judgment is always right. How often in my willfulness have I complained against You! Deal mercifully with me, O Lord, and teach me Your will in my regard.—Grant, O Lord, that I may walk undefiled through my way in life, seeking to walk according to Your will, as marked out for me by my holy rule, for I know that this is Your law for me."

Abbot Smith says that all of Psalm 118 is in praise of the simple, direct life of the religious who is devoted to the praises of God and who is subjected to rule, in order to become blameless before God. The music of the Introit resembles many other compositions of Mode I (see *Suscepimus* for Feb. 2, and compare the music of today's *judicium tuum* with the *misericordiam tuam* of that feast). *Justus* here is not the clarion call which is usual in this phrase, but rather a simple statement of God's justice, which *Domine* brings down to us. *Et rectum* is higher, because God's justice comes to us from His judgment seat in heaven. In *fac cum servo tuo* it seems as if the singer is asking that he be taken up to God, in order that he might judge with God's judgment. In singing the phrase, if it is necessary for the choir to take a breath, it would seem better to do so after *secundum* rather than before it, and thus keep the sequence of the music moving naturally.

GRADUAL — Psalm 32:12,6.

"Bless me, O Lord, for I am Your child; You are my Lord God. I am Your inheritance, and You have chosen me. Of myself I am worthless, but of great value if, by Your grace, I am faithful to You. You are great and powerful, O Lord, the Creator of all things by Your word."

Beata gens give us the picture of a people being raised up to God; it is quiet blessedness, because we have gone step by step up to God, *cujus est Dominus,* and *Deus eorum* has come down to us. The *populus quem elegit*—and we hope we are among those who have been chosen—are living a life that keeps them close to God in heaven. In the music for *Dominus in hereditatem sibi* we are reminded that we became heirs of God because He came down from heaven to die for us and to open heaven, our inheritance. The *verbo Domini* in heaven created the heavens, and *oris ejus,* the words of His mouth which gave power to all (*omnis*), still remain a power to us to do all things which He has commanded.

ALLELUIA – Psalm 101:2.

"Hear my prayer, O Lord, and let my cry of distress come unto You."

The word *Domine* is a simple, reverent approach, but the *exaudi* is like an anguished cry; *orationem meam* is but a simple prayer, one asking for mercy; but now *clamor* takes on something of the appeal that was found in *exaudi,* and the *veniat* comes up to the throne of grace, of mercy.

In the Gospel we find the beautiful answer to the prayer we have been singing: "Your prayer will be heard if you remember the first and greatest commandment: Love God." So we are able to make the words of Daniel our own as we sing:

OFFERTORY – Daniel 9:17,18,19.

"I, Daniel, prayed to my God; and I said: O Lord, hear the prayer of Your servant; show that You are here present in the sanctuary; and look with favor upon Your people, O God, over whom I have called Your blessing." This is the first instance we have of the inspired writer telling his own name at the beginning of a prayer.

In *oravi* we can see the humble, prayerful attitude of the prophet, lifting his eyes to *Deum.* There is humility in *ego,* but the ascending notes for the last syllable of *Daniel* seem to say that the prophet is close to God only because of God's mercy. The music for *dicens* leads easily into the body of the prayer in which each of the words seems to be aptly illustrated by the notes to be sung. The last word, *Deus*, is a beautiful melody in itself, full of adoration, love, and petition.

The Offertory seems to say to us: "Here, in Daniel, you will see one of God's servants whose whole service was an offering of love. Before you offer your gifts at the Offertory, look into your heart and see if you, too, are offering a similar service to God."

COMMUNION – Psalm 75:12,13.

"You people of God, make your vows to Him as a recognition of His right over you; and let each soul offer to God what is His due. Bring Him presents, especially you who are near His tabernacle. Remember to be reverent before Him, for He can humble the pride of princes; He can crush even the kings of the earth." This Communion hymn, too, reminds us that by the vows we have made to God we owe Him more than others.

Here again, as in the Introit, we have a picture of the just Judge. It is unusual to find such serious words used in the Communion, but it seems to be the Church's mind to keep injecting the idea of the end of the world and judgment. We have just received the sacrament of Love; surely the psalm will make the words less serious in their aspect, but they will remind us, too, of the part that love can play. If our hearts (our love) were in the presents we (who dwell nearer the tabernacle than others) offered before the consecration, then we need have no fear—we know not fear because of our love.

The music is a simple melody, but a reverent one. Notice the simplicity of the music for *Domino Deo vestro*: make your offerings purely, simply, to the Lord your God. *In circuitu* is a picture of those dwelling around the tabernacle, and in *affertis munera* we have the raising of hands filled with gifts. *Terribili* sounds more terrible in the first instance; in the second, it is more like the sure fate that awaits those who try to usurp divine power, and symbolizes the downfall of such kings.

EIGHTEENTH
SUNDAY AFTER PENTECOST

There is an expectancy, an awaiting, in the liturgy of today. The end of the year is approaching, and then will come Advent, when the long-awaited One will be welcomed.

INTROIT – Sir. 36:18; Psalm 121:1.

"To them that patiently wait for You, O Lord, grant them peace; that Your prophets (who foretold Your coming) may be found faithful to the promises they gave. O Lord, hear the prayer of Your servant, and of Your holy people.—As soon as I learn to trust You, my Lord, community life becomes a joy, for I recognize the goodness of those who live with me, and we go together into your house."

The music of *Da pacem, Domine* is a heartfelt cry, but not anguished. It seems rather a cry of patience while waiting, rather than for peace amid confusion; that idea is prevalent, too, in the patient tone of *sustinentibus*. *Fideles* seems to indicate a fidelity regarding the promises they told us concerning God's coming, as though they lifted up our hearts with their promises. *Exaudi preces* once more seems to indicate the request that God should bend down to hear not only our prayer, but that of all His faithful all over the world (*et plebs tuae Israel*).

The Collect prays that God may direct our hearts while we wait for His coming, and the Letter to the Corinthians speaks of the gratitude of St. Paul for his people who have been enriched in Christ, and made so firm that they lacked no grace "while awaiting the appearance of our Lord Jesus Christ."

GRADUAL – Psalm 121:1,7.

Today's Gradual also appeared on the fourth Sunday of Lent (*Laetare*) where an explanation of it has been given (page 50).

ALLELUIA – Psalm 101:16.

"Your kindness to me, O Lord, will make those who forget You have reverence for You; and the rulers of this darkness, the evil spirits, will acknowledge Your glory." The music for *timebunt gentes* is like a child speaking of some punishment to come, but in *nomen tuum* we can picture (Phil. 2): "At the Name of

135

Jesus every knee shall bend, of those in heaven, on earth, and
under the earth." In *omnes reges* is pictured the great rulers of
nations, who shall bow down to the earth in adoration before
the one, true God. It is almost a promise of the Magi adoring
the infant King.

There is an interesting picture in the Gospel story today
which could easily be lost sight of; it is contained in the words:
"...they brought to Him a paralytic...and Jesus saw *their* faith."
Evidently, the friends of the young man are the ones who brought
him to Christ, and because of *their* faith, our Lord performed the
miracle of absolution and healing (health of soul before health
of body). It was *their* watchfulness which was rewarded.

OFFERTORY – Ex. 24:4,5.

We are reminded of the opportunity we are now to have,
the privilege of making our offering: "Moses consecrated an altar
to the Lord, offering upon it sacrifice, the sacrifice of victims; he
made an evening sacrifice to the Lord God for an odor of sweetness, before the eyes of the children of Israel." In offering this
sacrifice, the Secret says, we become "partakers of the supreme
Godhead."

The music throughout this beautiful Offertory hymn pictures
the heights reached by those who offer themselves (*immolans vic-
timas*). One writer has said that *sacrificium vespertinum* refers to
the Sacrifice of Christ at the ninth (vesper) hour, but I am one
of those who hope it may prefigure the privilege of offering the
holy Sacrifice in the evening for the benefit of those who would
but cannot attend the morning Sacrifice. How that odor of sweetness (*odorem suavitatis*) would arise to the highest heavens if this
were made possible! Let it be an intention in your prayer today,
so that soon all people, of all stations (*filiorum Israel*) may have
the daily opportunity of lifting themselves high before the face
(*in conspectu*) of God by their union in His Sacrifice. Then, too,
may more voices be able to join us in the sublime song of the

COMMUNION – Psalm 95:8,9.

"My poor offerings will I offer to You, O Lord, and these
will make my adoration of You generous in Your sight. In the
choir and in the sanctuary I will adore You, as in the courts of
heaven." This is a beautiful, a happy song, which starts off fear-

lessly, gladly, willingly, to bring one closer to God. All this is expressed in the first seven words, followed by the picture of adoration in *adorate Dominum*, and concludes with the heavenly picture of *in aula sancta ejus*.

The expectancy, the awaiting shall indeed be rewarded beyond all merit of ours.

NINETEENTH
SUNDAY AFTER PENTECOST

The theme of today's liturgy seems to be one of fidelity. This thought begins with the Introit, and is evident in every other part of the liturgy today.

INTROIT

"If you are faithful to me," says God, "keeping well the commands I have given you, I shall be the salvation of the people. Turn to Me when you have tribulations, and according to the manner in which you have preserved the wedding garment of grace within your soul, I will hear you and be your Lord." *Psalm 77:1:* "O all you who are friends of the Lord, take to heart the law He has given you; bow down to your ears to His gentle voice, and your wills to His will."

Christ who lived among men on earth was a solace to them, lifting them above the things of the earth *salus populi*; and the *ego sum* reminds us of His coming down from heaven to dwell on earth with us. There is a spirit of very reverent awe in the music of *dicit Dominus*, as if we were saying; "Imagine, God has told us this Himself." Whenever we are being tried, if we lift our voices to Him (*tribulatione clamaverint*), He will open His Heart to our prayer and stoop down (*exaudiam eos*) to help us. Note the similarity in the music of *clamaverint ad me* and *exaudiam eos*. The music of *ero illorum Dominus* continues the promise to come down among men and help them, and *in perpetuum* seems to tell us that He will do both in heaven and on earth.

In the Collect we pray that God will ever keep us from all that would draw us away from Him, and St. Paul, in the Epistle, tells us how we ourselves must act in order to deserve this help from God.

GRADUAL – Psalm 140:2.

"May my prayer, O Lord, rise to You as incense offered at the altar rises, and may my hands be ever lifted up to You as an evening sacrifice" (i.e., in thanksgiving). We express the thought that we want to be faithful, and we ask God to look graciously on our prayers for this intention.

Dirigatur is like a call to God asking for His advice, and then immediately my prayer (*oratio mea*) rises, step by step, to Him. The music of *sicut incensum* is like a wisp of smoke curling up before the face (*conspectu*) of God, who, pleased with the sacrifice we offer, comes down to dwell among us. The notes on the words *elevatio manuum* and *sacrificium vespertinum* give a beautiful picture of hands raised to heaven in supplication. The hands of the priest, extended during the holy Sacrifice, remind us of Moses praying on the mountain top that God's army may be victorious over the enemy. Moses grew weary, and when his arms dropped from time to time, two young men were called to come and hold up his hands as he prayed. The ascent and descent of the music in the Gradual bring back that picture also.

ALLELUIA – Psalm 104:1.

"I do give thanks to You, my Lord, and I will call upon Your Name; I will make known your wonderful works to the nations which know You not."

The *Alleluia* is truly a joyous one, a far echo of Easter Sunday's *Confitemini*, and the music of the first six words that follow is full of the happiness which fills the soul of one who realizes what a privilege it is to be allowed to call upon God's Name. *Annuntiate gentes* give us a foreign-mission picture of going far and wide among those who do not know God. The last seven notes of *annuntiate* sound like a missioner repeating and emphasizing his instructions: *doh la, doh la, doh sol sol.* Missioners at home need have no feeling that they cannot share the active apostolate when they have such hymns with which to emphasize their petitions for missioners afar. *Opera ejus* reminds us of the joy we have in doing God's work, no matter where on earth we may be.

The Gospel of the wedding feast tells us what happens to those who are not clothed with the robe of grace, and so in the Offertory we pray that such a thing may never happen to us.

OFFERTORY – Psalm 137:7.

"I know, O Lord, that if I should ever be in trouble again, You will give me the strength of soul I need to see me through it; You will protect me from the enemies of my soul with Your strong right hand, for it is only Your strength which has saved me in the past."

The music of the whole Offertory is symbolic of uplifted hands, as in the Alleluia verse. There is only one place where a great simplicity occurs, and that is on the words *et salvum me fecit*. If I were directing a choir, I would ask them to sing those words strongly, and much more slowly. The prayer of the Post-communion asks for the grace that we may ever hold fast to the commandments. It is a fitting prayer to follow the simple hymn of the Communion.

COMMUNION – Psalm 118:4,5.

"I will keep Your commandments with all diligence, O Lord; direct my ways, and allow me to follow the perfection to which You have called me."

The whole hymn should be sung thoughtfully and not too hurriedly. The accidental which appears so often adds a little note of sadness to the piece. The soul has just been refreshed with the Body of Christ, and with Him resting so near the heart, there comes the realization that, in the past, we have not always done the things commanded us. We have failed, we have been without the wedding garment; and yet the sadness is mingled with joy, because we were not cast out into exterior darkness, but were taken back into the Heart of our God, through His great mercy towards us. This seems emphasized by the similarity which occurs in *custodiendas* and *justificationes*.

TWENTIETH
SUNDAY AFTER PENTECOST

In spite of the words of the Offertory verse, this is a very happy Sunday. We shall see, too, that even the Offertory is full of happiness. The happiness which St. Paul urges in the Epistle must be founded on faith: we have been privileged above many, through no desserts of our own, to receive the glorious gift of faith. The royal official mentioned in the Gospel shows us what he did when the same gift came to him—he shared his gift with so many others. That is the second reason for happiness today—that we are privileged by our baptism (and this is true of all who have been baptized) to be God's instruments, no matter where we are, no matter what our place in life, in sharing our soul's happiness with others by bringing them the glad tidings of the Gospel, either in person, or by our prayers and example.

INTROIT – Daniel 3:31,29,35; Psalm 118:1.

"All that You have done to us, O Lord, You have done in true judgment, because we have sinned against You and have not obeyed Your commandments; we pray that glory may be given Your great mercy. Grant, O Lord, that I may be undefiled in my way through life, seeking to walk according to Your will, as marked out for me by my holy Rule, for I know that this is Your law for me."

Just a glance at the music of the Introit shows us what a simple, joyous song it is. Notice the simplicity of all until we come to the word *Domine*, and again when we come to *fecisti*. The music for *quia* seems a little hesitant, as if we are ashamed to excuse ourselves when we realize that our sin has been an insult to the most high God (*tibi*). In *da gloriam nomini* we see the offering of all things to God in heaven. At *et fac* we have a repetition of the first notes, but in the music that follows there is a tendency to be a little more florid in praising God for the mercies which have come down to us.

GRADUAL – Psalm 144:15-16.

This Gradual has already been explained on the feast of Corpus Christi. Our Lord in the holy Eucharist is the center of our faith, bringing us in the Blessed Sacrament the peace and pardon we ask for in today's Collect. That may be one reason why this Gradual is repeated today.

ALLELUIA — Psalm 107:2.

"Make my heart ready to turn to You in any danger, O my God; let me sing a psalm to Your glory and mercy." These words are set to the same melody found on the fourth Sunday of Advent. On that Sunday we said that the music on the first word was almost shy; in today's liturgy we can see the same thing, but it is shyness resulting from the awe we feel that God has made our hearts ready. The repetition of the words carries a more joyous melody as we begin to realize what God has made our hearts ready for. And so our voices rise and fall in spiritual canticles as we try to spread His glory to all the ends of the earth.

OFFERTORY — Psalm 136:1.

"When I was bound by the chain of sin, O Lord, I was sad; but then I remembered Your home in heaven which You had designed for my delight."

The rivers of sinful attachments (*Super flumina Babylonis*) graphically wind in and out, up and down, and *illic sedimus* gives a picture as if someone were rocking back and forth in woe, while *flevimus* surely brings us down into the valley of tears. But then our faith reminds us that heaven awaits faithful souls.

COMMUNION — Psalm 118:49,50.

"O Lord, You have given me a strong hope. Mindful of Your promises, fulfill this hope in me, Your servant. In my deepest humiliations, when I seemed nearest dead in Your service, my hope in You has been my consolation."

The music of this Communion hymn is almost hushed in its simplicity. It is very much like a person speaking to a dear friend, reminding him of a promise made. It is one of the finest examples in music of the truth that "prayer is familiar conversation with God." May the happiness which springs from our faith be augmented as we do all in our power to pass on to others not only our faith, but something of the happiness, that foretaste of heaven, which comes to the hearts of those who can humbly say, "Lord, I do believe; help Thou my unbelief."

TWENTY-FIRST
SUNDAY AFTER PENTECOST

The beatitudes, which comprise the Gospel on November 1, seem to be the keynote of today's liturgy: "Blessed are the clean of heart, the merciful, the peace-makers, and they who suffer persecution for My sake." From the Introit through the Communion-psalm runs the thread of blessedness which may be attained in spite of temptations, torments, and persecution.

INTROIT − Esther 13:9,10-11; Psalm 118:1.

"All things are under Your will, O Lord, and there is none to resist Your will: for You have made all things, heaven and earth, and all the things under the vault of heaven.—Grant, O Lord, that I may be undefiled in my way through life, seeking to walk according to Your will, as marked out for me by my holy Rule, for I know this is Your law for me."

This beautiful prayer from the Book of Esther is that of Mardochai, who addresses almighty God in this manner after having refused to give honor to any but the true God. He is mercifully released from death because of the mercy he had already shown to others. The music is simple, befitting the humble words. It begins almost recitatively stating a fact, and then as it grows in fervor (*et non est qui*) the music takes on a happier aspect. Once more *coelum et terram*...returns to the original theme, rising with the thought that all that exists under heaven is the work of God's hand. The music of this Introit contains a beautiful motif for a prayerful, dignified processional.

It is possible that the Apostle to the Gentiles had Mardochai in mind when he wrote today's letter to the Ephesians. God has always befriended those who "put on the armor of God." And so we pray in the Gradual: "may we find all our defense in Him."

GRADUAL − Psalm 89:1-2.

"You are ever the refuge of those who serve You, O Lord. Your kindness is manifested, because the fleeting years of man's life are as nothing to Your eternity. Before the mountains were made and stood up out of the waters, You were God."

The music of this Gradual is familiar, not only because of its appearance in the Requiem Mass, but also on the first Sunday of Lent, Easter, and in the Mass of Sts. Simon and Jude.

Today's introduction of the *Domine* is similar to the humble introduction of the Introit. Some liturgists believe that we should not look for tone-painting in this hymn, but it seems that whoever set the texts to this music had in mind the oneness of an idea which fits the music in each instance.

Refugium factus es nobis gives us a picture of God's loving protection placed around us, and a *generatione et progenie* portrays the extent of God's mercy (see *ut custodiant*...on the first Sunday of Lent and *et lux*...in the Requiem). Just as we saw God's hands lifting man up (first Sunday of Lent) and can see His eternal love (Requiem), so here the application of *montes* to the music gives us a picture of the eternal hills rising out of the waters. *Saecula* shows again the extent of God's mercy; the picture of God (*Deus*) still reigning at the end is very beautiful. This Gradual occurs usually towards the end of October or in November, and it may be that the music was used to remind us to pray for the dead: the measure of our mercy towards the Poor Souls will be that which is meted out to us one day.

ALLELUIA – Psalm 113:1.

"(When) Israel came out of Egypt, the house of Jacob fled from among a strange people (Your people, O Lord, by Your kindness, became Your sanctuary)."

At first sight it would seem that the Alleluia verse is a *non sequitur*, but with the thought of All Soul's Day in mind, there may be a connection, since this psalm is sung at funerals in some parts of the world. To the arranger of the liturgy this may have been an apt addition. Then, too, we can see in it the connection that God is the refuge not only of all nations, but of each individual nation that will turn to Him and acknowledge Him as its God. There is no limit to God's eternal mercy.

OFFERTORY – Job 1:2.

"There was a man in the land whose name was Job, simple and upright and fearing God, whom Satan tried to tempt; and power was given him from the Lord over Job's possessions and his flesh, and he destroyed all his substance and his children, and wounded Job's flesh with a malignant ulcer."

The definition of mercy is, "compassion for the unfortunate," and so we have *cum* and *patio* (to suffer together with). Our hearts go out to the holy man Job in his sufferings, and we pray, as we make our offering to God, that whatever it may cost us to sacrifice our wills, we may have the faith that was Job's, who trusted completely in God. The music is picturesque throughout. The introduction, again, has the simplicity of the two preceding hymns we have sung. See the picture in the music of *simplex* and *rectus*; see also the power given by God to Satan in *potestas a Domino*. The music for *carnem quoque* to the end is truly compassionate.

COMMUNION – Psalm 118:81,84,86.

"My soul has longed for Your salvation, O my God, and I wait with great hope that Your promises may be fulfilled; how long shall I be subject to the enemies of my soul, the evil ones who try to disturb me and draw me away from You? O Lord, my God, help me!"

Following the Offertory, it is easy to see the application of Job's sufferings to our own condition; and following the reception of holy Communion, it is still easier to see, as Job did, that all our help lies in God's mercy to us. The music of this hymn is beautiful in its simplicity. Notice the simple introduction again, and how this is carried out in the whole piece except on the words *speravi, judicum*, and *Domine Deus. Iniqui persecuti...Domine* begins like a psalm tone, but it could be used as a beautiful prayer for help in the moment of temptation.

May today's liturgy remind us of Portia's words (*Merchant of Venice*): "The quality of mercy is...twice bless'd: it blesses him that gives, and him that takes; mercy...is an attribute to God Himself." Shakespeare knew the beatitudes.

TWENTY-SECOND
SUNDAY AFTER PENTECOST

As we approach the end of the liturgical year, the theme of our singing today might be taken as a prayer that we may continue to grow each day more and more in love, in order that we may think only of becoming more pleasing to no one but God. Monsignor Knox's translation of St. Paul's Epistle to the Philippians will be our reminder: "I am confident that He who has inspired generosity in you will bring it to perfection, ready for the day when Jesus Christ comes. It is only fitting that I should entertain such hopes for you: you are close to my heart, and I know that you all share my happiness in being a prisoner, and being able to assert and defend the truth of the Gospel. God knows how I long for you all, with the tenderness of Jesus Christ Himself. And this is my prayer for you: may your love grow richer and richer yet, in the fulness of its knowledge and the depth of its perception, so that you may learn to prize what is of value; may nothing cloud your conscience or hinder your progress until the day when Christ comes; may you reap through Jesus Christ the full harvest of your justification to God's glory and praise."

INTROIT – Psalm 129:3,4,1-2.

The Introit begins with verse 3, but Abbot Smith's paraphrase of the first four verses gives us the complete thought put into this beautiful prayer: (1) "Out of the depths of my own selfishness I have cried to You, O Lord. Hear my voice. (2) Be ever attentive to me, Lord. Ah, how little need there has been in the past to attend to my cry, for I have not called to You. I did not look to You for help. (3) Attend to me doubly now, that I may turn to You. I have delayed too long. Wait for me now, a little, O Lord; I am so slow. (4) I know You are all mercy. I need much mercy and forgiveness. O Lord, my God, I will await Your time, only make me constant."

The music approaches God directly, pleadingly, as if to ask Him now to look down (*observaveris*) from His place in heaven. In the next phrase, the insistent cry reaching up to God reminds us of heaven's judgment concerning sin; *propitiatio* is a humble call for mercy, and *Deus Israel* is very fervent, as if to say that we realize that only the God who was so kind to Israel is the One to whom we look for help, too. It is the memory of His mercies in the past which stirs up greater love in our hearts.

GRADUAL — Psalm 132:1-2.

"I begin to see, O Lord, how great a good for my soul, and how full of joy it is, that You have called me to dwell in a community united in their ranks with Your Son, my Lord Jesus Christ. As the precious ointment that You commanded to be poured so copiously upon the head of Your chosen priest Aaron that it flowed upon his beard, signifying the strength, the joy, and the sweet savor of the consecration of Your priests, so the mutual charity found in a religious community will bring strength, and joy, and a sweet odor pleasing to You."

Look back at the Epistle quoted above, and see how aptly this Gradual follows the thought expressed there. The music of *Ecce* seems to say, "But look, here is a wonderful thing!" We know from experience how wonderful a thing unity is in a religious community, and so it would be well for us to pray today as we sing this, that that same unity may exist in the parishes and cathedrals where this is chanted today, that all who attend the holy Sacrifice today may understand the joy of being firmly united under God. The *habitare* shows that one day we hope to be dwelling together in heaven; why not begin that unity on earth? *Unguentem* gives us a picture of the oil flowing high upon the head (*capite*) and from that height down upon the beard (*barbam*) of the priest. Two Sundays ago (twentieth after Pentecost) we sang the music which we have today on the word *Aaron*—it is the melody for the word *mea* at the end of the Alleluia verse on that Sunday.

ALLELUIA — Psalm 113:11.

"They who fear You, O Lord, hope in You; You are their helper and protector." The music for today's Alleluia and verse is the same as that sung on the sixteenth Sunday after Pentecost. It seems more applicable to the words of that Sunday than today's, but we may find a parallel in the thought: those who hope in the Lord are prompted to do so because of their love, and so they, too, sing of the wonderful things God does for those who prove their love of Him.

OFFERTORY – Esther 14:12,13.

"Be mindful of me, O Lord. You are the ruler above all rulers. Give to my mouth well-chosen words, that what I have to say may be pleasing in the sight of the Prince." This beautiful prayer was uttered by Esther, as she was about to appear before the king to plead for her people. We can make this same prayer ours.

The music throughout this Offertory is a simple, reverent setting for this fine prayer. The most striking part of the whole piece is the music on *in conspectu principis*. It is like a slow, dignified, but sufficiently humble address to a King. Esther teaches us here how to make our offering to God, for in proportion as we offer ourselves to Him, we receive His return of Love, and thus we become more pleasing to Him.

COMMUNION – Psalm 16:6.

"O God, I have besought You to hear me, and You have graciously listened to me. Bend down Your ear still to me, O my God." This is one of the most beautiful pieces of music in all the liturgy. It is direct and full of life, yet at the same time there is much fervor in all of it. *Ego clamavi*—"I, a creature of earth, have dared to lift my voice to You, O God, asking You to look down on me." And God heard in heaven (*exaudisti*), encouraging me to lift my voice still higher to reach His ear (*inclina aurem tuam*) until He bent down His ear to hear my lowly words (*verba mea*).

Today's liturgy fills us with confidence. If we grow richer in the knowledge and love of God, a generosity will fill our lives—generosity in our service both to God and to men for love of Him—and so nothing will hinder our progress until the day when the Lord shall come.

TWENTY-THIRD
SUNDAY AFTER PENTECOST

The theme of this Sunday may be found in our Lord's words: "Ah, if you could but understand the ways that lead to peace" (Luke 19:42).

INTROIT – Jeremias 29:11,12,14; Psalm 84:2.

"The Lord said: I think thoughts of peace and not of disturbance; call upon Me and I will listen to you, and I will redeem you from the captivity you are in, wherever you may be.—How good You have been to me, O my God; you have blessed me and freed me from the captivity of the world." The words of Jeremias introduce the motif of today's liturgy.

The dignity of *Dicit Dominus* is very beautiful, as if the resonant voice of Jeremias was reminding us that these were not his words, but God's. The simplicity of *Ego cogito* leads us fearlessly to listen to His words; it is the voice of a kind, compassionate Father. See how God's peace (*pacis*) can lift us up to Him. *Invocabitis me* is like a gentle invitation to tell our troubles to the Father; and the *exaudiam* seems to say that He will be in no hurry for us to finish, but will give us plenty of time to talk with Him. See the simplicity of being released as captives (*reducam...*) when it is God who comes to our assistance.

Many people seem to have no peace in their lives. They worry about wars, prophecies, dire forebodings, and here all the time God is waiting to assure them that His peace is the only thing that can relieve worry and concern. There's a lot of pride in worry—WE can't see how a thing can be done or undone. God knows and He tells us today, so that we may remember it. That is why the Collect prays that He will always release us from the captivity which sin is. St. Paul, too, in his Epistle reminds the Philippians that those who forget to turn to God in life will have difficulty in finding God turned toward them at the end.

Poor St. Paul had an Evodia and Syntche to scold, too. His appeal to them to be peaceable is well worded: "Be ye of one mind!" That is an echo of last Sunday's "*quam bonum.*" We realize, though, how often and how patiently God has helped us over the difficulties which appeared in our path; how He has brought peace into our lives when there seemed to be no peace; so we sing in the

GRADUAL — Psalm 43:8-9.

"When the enemies of the soul assaulted me, O Lord, I trusted in You alone for deliverance. You reduced them to shame. All the days of my life, my glory is in You, my God; let me praise You now and always." This hymn begins simply, but becomes a little more elaborate as it progresses from *Domine* through *affligentibus* until it comes to *confudisti. Eos qui nos oderunt* are evidently not very nice people, so they are not given any special attention. *Deo* seems to be unusually extended, but in singing God's Name, the soul does not wish ever to stop praising it. Notice, too, how *tota die* and *in saecula* picture the length of time which the soul would spend praising God.

On the third Sunday of Advent, in the Gradual, the words *qui regis* are sung to the same melody as *Deo* above.

ALLELUIA — Psalm 129:1-2.

"Out of the depths I have cried to You, O Lord. Hear my voice." In today's Alleluia, the third division of the music is a repetition of the second. We might think of it as an echo, and here, and again on *vocem meam*, it could be sung a little more softly. The *De profundis* melody here is almost a happy one, as if we realized that it is only because of God's goodness that we have been lifted up. *Clamavi* and *ad te* reach up to God, but *Domine* is very reverent. The next *Domine* is in praise of the Lord on high who in heaven heard (*exaudi*) the voice of one even so lowly as I (*vocem meam*).

OFFERTORY — Psalm 129:1-2.

The *De Profundis* is repeated, but the word *orationem* is used here instead of *vocem*. This melody is more solemn than that of the Alleluia verse. We have come to the part of the holy Sacrifice where we offer our gifts, and it is a time for serious reflection: we should have nothing to offer, had not God raised us up from great depths to lead our steps to Him. At one time, the second and third verses of the *De Profundis* were sung in this Offertory, and after each verse the first verse was repeated again, and finally at the end. That repetition of those words is very emphatic.

COMMUNION – Mark 11:24.

"I tell you that when you ask for anything in prayer, you have only to believe it is yours and it will be granted you." Ordinarily this Communion hymn is sung too fast. It should not be, since we realize that God is speaking to us; it should not be dragged, but sung majestically, quietly, as God would speak. The music of this song is easily understood; it fits the words so precisely. The last three words are particularly beautiful.

This Communion seems to sum up all we have been saying about today's theme: "If you could but know..."; "call upon Me and I will listen..."; "when enemies of soul assault..."; "*clamavi ad te*..."; "*exaudi*...." While we are mindful of the fact that the end of the liturgical year symbolizes the end of life, the end of the world and judgment, yet there is before us today the realization that God will hear our prayers and will send His holy One to save us. Each Mass should remind us of this fact. Some one Mass will be the end of our mortal life; if we use each day's Sacrifice with that thought in mind, we shall be harvesting all that God has promised to those who love and serve Him.

SANCTORAL CYCLE

IMMACULATE CONCEPTION

December 8

This feast was not celebrated in the Church until after its definition in 1854; so it was not observed in the time of St. Gregory, and he could not have written the music for the feast itself. Yet he did write the music that we sing today. The Introit melody was originally written for the fifth Sunday after Easter. I could not discover whether the connection between the words of both Introits inspired today's use of it, but see the strong parallel: "Adore God, all you His angels: Sion heard and was glad; and the daughters of Judah rejoiced" (5th Sunday after Easter). *Adore God* is always used as an exclamation of joy, very much as *Praise God* is a religious exclamation today. Why praise or adore Him? Because one of the daughters of Judah has been favored from the moment of her conception. So our Lady, as though knowing that psalm, says her first *Magnificat* in today's

INTROIT – Isaias 61:10.

Her first Magnificat	*Her later Magnificat*
I will greatly rejoice in the Lord and my soul shall be joyful in my God.	My soul magnifies the Lord.
For He has clothed me with the garments of salvation...as a bride adorned with jewels.	For He has done great things for me.
I will extol Thee, O Lord, for Thou hast upheld me and not let my enemies rejoice over me.	He has shown might in His arm.

We make her words our own today, since God has so favored "our tainted nature's solitary boast." Therefore, the Introit must be sung sincerely, with solemnity, yet with a joy that emanates from souls elevated to a high place near God. Notice how quietly the song of joy begins—joy that is not satisfied with earth but reaches up into heaven. Let us rejoice in the Lord—and the *Domino* almost chuckles, as do the next three words. They strive to maintain the exultation of soul. Then, very reverently, we understand why: all this is made possible for us *in Deo meo*. It's the realization that all the grace with which we are vested makes us go to such heights, singing of "the robe of salvation." The music of *et indumento* parallels the opening phrase, as if to recall "This is why I shall rejoice." Note the earthiness of *sponsam*; but how beautiful our souls become as they rise from earth, adorned with the jewels of sanctifying grace.

GRADUAL — Judith 13:23; 15:10.

The music, like that of the Introit, of necessity had to be borrowed. It was written originally for the feast of Sts. Peter and Paul, where the words find another parallel to those of today's Mass:

You, O Lord, shall make them to be princes over all the earth.	You are blessed, O Princess Mary, by the Most High God above all the women of the earth.... You are the honor of our people.

The Introit's words were our Lady's; the Gradual's are ours. This is one of the most gloriously lilting melodies in the whole *Liber*. It should be sung lightly, airily, in not too low a key. It must be the expression of what the soul feels at being able to say these things to Mary: "Today you are blessed, dear Mother! But by your favor, when I shed this mortality, may I, too, rise to great heights."

There is much reverence in the music of the first words: *Virgo Maria* is like a silken banner waving in the breeze; then the ascent to God (*excelso*). *Super* stays up as it should, but see the descent to earth in *terram*. It is always better to be close to God. We must, unfortunately, come down to earth at times, but that makes the next ascent even more pleasant. The adaptation of *Tu gloria* is easily seen. *Israel* is very low, because it was from the soil of Israel that Mary was lifted up to be the honor of her people. The *Alleluia* joy is repeated in *tota pulchra*, but the *et macula originalis* is almost breathless surprise, for such a thing has never been heard of before or since. *Non est* takes up the strain of the *Alleluia*, like a beautiful refrain that perforce repeats itself.

What was said of the *Ave Maria* in the Preface also holds true for this

OFFERTORY – Luke 1:28.

The only difference is that, because of the occasion, we are not quite so direct in singing these notes. This is a "dress up" occasion, very formal, because we want to show more than everyday honor.

COMMUNION

The music is the same as that in the Mass for Several Martyrs: "I tell you, my friends, do not be afraid of those who persecute you." Today's Communion tells why: "for He who is mighty...." This is a very serene, comforting composition, as if to tell us: "Be calm! The things that are told of your Mother Mary are for your comfort. He, the Mighty One, who has done great things for her because of her fidelity, will do great things for you, also, if you honor her by imitation."

Note the reverence in *Maria*; the stooping down of God, *tibi*; the magnitude of *magna*; the mystery of *potens est*. How well we should sing this Communion! Our Lord has just come down from heaven to enter our souls, in order that He may do great things for us, too.

ASSUMPTION

August 15

In Japan, on this day, there is a feast which honors all who have died. The farmers have finished with their rice crops and can visualize a good harvest, so three days of relaxation are enjoyed. Now all the people take advantage of the occasion, and there is a spirit of quiet, joyful rest. Some have tried to see a connection between today's feast and the Oriental holiday, and not a few missioners are taking advantage of the latter to introduce the former.

The observance of the holy day is for us a brief respite in the midst of summer, and we are refreshed by the promise implied in our Lady's having been taken up into heaven.

INTROIT – Apocalypse 12:1; Psalm 97:1.

"A great portent appeared in heaven: a woman wearing the sun for her mantle, with the moon under her feet, and a crown of twelve stars about her head.—Sing to the Lord a new song, a song of wonder at His doings."

The picture given in the words of the Apocalypse is truly awesome, and the music for the Introit seems to carry this idea throughout. Only at *apparuit*, and again at *in capite*, does the music reach a moderate height. Notice the reserved tone of *corona* and *-odecim*, while the twelve notes on *(stell)arum du-* seem to cluster about our Lady's head. The gladness of the psalm tone expresses the joy of children who are so proud of the honor accorded to their Mother. We may recall the joy we experienced at our Lord's ascension; today we are doubly assured that both our Mother and her divine Son will one day lift us up to a place with them, if we continue serving them in love.

GRADUAL – Psalm 44:11-12,14.

"Listen, my daughter, and give ear attentively to my words: your beauty is for the king's delight. She comes, the princess all fair to see, to meet the king, her robe of golden cloth." Alleluia: "As Mary is assumed into heaven, the army of angels rejoices."

The music of the first words sounds like a strict command, but it is followed by a glorious passage of music which points out the beauty of heaven. Then *inclina* and *aurem tuam* seem to represent the acts of bending down one's ear to catch the words falling from heaven. At *rex* we look up again to the eternal King who seems, in the music of *pulchritudinem tuam*, to lavishly praise the beauty of his virgin daughter and Mother.

Tota decora is surely fair to see, both in the arrangement of notes and in the melody itself. *Ingreditur filia* seems to show a grateful entrance, and a curtsy to the king (*regis*). The texture of gold (*texturae aureae*) is expressed without boasting, but *amictus ejus* gives a fine picture of the graceful folds of the gown which adorns the queen. The rising and descending notes of *Alleluia* also carry out the idea of being assumed into heaven from earth, while the *assumpta est* is rendered in a somewhat matter-of-fact manner—it is only natural that our Lady, because of her great virtues, should be taken bodily into heaven! The *gaudet* and *ange-lorum* carry out the swelling joy of the *Alleluia*. How our hearts should swell with joyful pride at this *Alleluia*: it is our Mother Mary who has been so beautifully praised!

OFFERTORY – Genesis 3:15.

"The Lord God said to the serpent, 'I will establish a feud between you and the woman, between your offspring and hers.' " A hymn in the Office of the Blessed Virgin, *Ave Maris Stella*, refers to this: "Gabriel used the name of Eva, changing it to Ave, so that God's Mother would bring peace to men's souls."

The music on *inimicitias* is symbolic of an anathema, while *ponam* seems to express that the power to do so comes from above. *Inter te* is very strong, but there seems to be a softening of God's wrath as we sing *et mulierem*. The remaining music is unusual but may be considered symbolic of the great number to be born and redeemed through the mediation of Mary. The contrast to all the other music in this Mass may also remind us of this contrast: Eve was driven out of Paradise—Mary is assumed bodily into the heavenly Eden.

COMMUNION – Luke, 1:48-49.

"All generations will count me blessed, because He who is mighty has wrought for me His wonders." This is a simple, beautiful melody, carefully avoiding any sign of boasting. The *beatam* reaches up towards God who has wrought such a wonder as to ask Mary to be the Mother of His Son. *Omnes generationes* gives a simple picture of all people, both those of high and low rank; and the music of *mihi* seems like surprising news—"to me!" We could sing this chant every morning of our lives, after we receive Mary's Son in holy Communion. Indeed, all people could say that we are blessed at such a moment, because the omnipotent God has wrought a great mystery of His love in our souls. Today we might ask our Mother to intercede for us that we may always keep our eyes, our hearts, our souls above the earth, so that one day we may be found worthy to be truly lifted up on high to the throne of God with Mary.

CHRIST THE KING
Last Sunday in October

It was necessary to take melodies from other sources and apply them to the texts used for this feast, which was not introduced until 1925. One can but marvel at the inspired way in which the chants already existing were adapted to the texts chosen for this day.

INTROIT — Apoc. 5:12; 1:6; Psalm 71:1.

"Power and Godhead, wisdom and strength, honor and glory and blessing (belong) by right (to) the Lamb that was slain; (may) blessing and power through endless ages be given to Him. —Grant to the King, O God, Your own skill in judgment, the inheritance of a throne."

The music begins in reverential dignity, lifting our eyes to the Lamb on the throne of God, leading us to *qui occisus est* with what might seem at first to be a mournful outburst, but in the light of redemption is a grateful song of joy. *Accipere virtutem* is almost matter-of-fact music, yet it actually enchances the glory which follows in *divinitatem*. The same idea seems to be found in *sapientiam et fortitudinem*, which brings us to the uplifting *honorem*. Once more our eyes are raised to the throne at *gloria et imperium*, and to the glory of eternity *in saecula saeculorum*.

Today all the members of Christ's Mystical Body stand in spirit before the throne of the King. That throne was, on Good Friday, the Cross; today it is the altar where the Lamb is present as truly in the holy Sacrifice as He was on the Tree nineteen hundred years ago. The gratitude that should fill our hearts is that spoken of by St. Paul in today's Epistle: "Give thanks to God the Father who has made us worthy to share the lot of the saints in light. He has rescued us from the power of darkness, and transferred us into the kingdom of His beloved Son, in whom we have our redemption through His Blood, the remission of our sins."

GRADUAL — Psalm 71:8,11.

"He shall rule from sea to sea, and from the river to the ends of the earth. And all kings of earth shall adore Him; all nations shall serve Him." *All kings shall adore Him*: our memory goes back to the feast of January 6, when three Oriental kings came to adore the new-born Christ. Hence, we find that those who arranged today's music were so mindful, too, and the music for the Gradual of our present feast is the same as that of Epiphany. Just as that music brightened that text, so, too, today we find: *Dominabitur* presenting our King raised in glory, ruling to such vast extents as shown in *usque ad mare*, and again *ad terminos orbis terrarum*. Note the invitation to lift up our eyes in adoration at the words *et adorabunt eum* that is given to us with our fellow members, the kings of the earth—we, who are still of the earth (*omnes reges terrae*). And we bow in adoration with all nations to serve Him (*servient eum*).

ALLELUIA — Daniel 7:14.

"His power, an eternal power, shall never be taken from Him, nor shall it ever be destroyed." The music for the Alleluia is taken from the fourth Sunday after Easter (second *Alleluia*). On that Sunday the verse read: "Christ, now that He has risen from the dead, cannot die any more; death has no power over Him." It may require a little extra time to do this, but compare those words with the words used in today's Mass; compare, too, the music for

Christus resurgens ex mortuis	with *potestas ejus potestas aeterna*;
jam non moritur	with *quae non afferetur*;
mors illa ultra...	with *et regnum ejus quod....*

Note the heavenly might which the music of *potestas* brings out in both instances, and then the simplicity of the statement that that power will never be taken away (*quae non auferetur*). Again, *et regnum ejus* pictures the glorious, eternal kingdom of God. Words from the *Credo*, *cujus regnum non erit finis*, could be sung to those same notes. Let those words remind us again, when we sing the *Credo* this morning, of the promise contained therein for each of us.

OFFERTORY — Psalm 2:8.

"Ask of Me and I will give you nations for your inheritance, and the ends of the earth for your possession." The words remind us of those words spoken by our Lord in his discourse at the Last Supper: "You have only to make any request of the Father in My Name, and He will grant it to you. Until now you have not been making any requests in My Name; make them, and they will be granted, to bring you gladness in full measure" (*John* 16; 23, 24). Note the last seven words: *to bring you gladness in full measure.* They show our Lord's desire to do everything He can to make our hearts happy as we serve Him in love.

The music of this Offertory is very calm, in spite of its extraordinary statement, but this only further emphasizes the power of our eternal King who is waiting for our asking, who is both willing and capable of fulfilling our every request. There have been few earthly kings so responsive to a people's request; only God waits in unending patience for our prayer and our love.

COMMUNION – Psalm 28:10,11.

The promise which lies in the words of the Communion contains the outstanding feature of today's feast: "The Lord is enthroned as King forever; the Lord shall bless His people with peace." The music for the first three words is dignified, but stately, as it should be; only at *in aeternum* does it rise to great heights of majesty, power, and glory. Then *Dominus benedicet* represents our prayer arising to God, and His blessing coming down to us (*populo suo*). The music on the last two words, *in pace*, gives promise of eternal peace; they should be sung, joyfully but slowly, as if we are loath to lose the savor of that blessed reward.

Joy should animate our souls on this beautiful feast because we, as members of Christ's Mystical Body, are trying to put into action the prayer we say so often daily, *Thy kingdom come.* That kingdom, the Preface today tells us, is "an eternal and universal kingdom; a kingdom of truth and life, a kingdom of holiness and grace, a kingdom of justice and love" and the only one of its kind in the world today: "a kingdom of peace." Pray that "your sacrifice and mine" today may reach out in God's Providence to draw all men's hearts to the eternal King of kings.

ALL SAINTS
November 1

Today's feast comes as the harvest season draws to a close, and it seems quite fitting that the harvest of saints should be honored at this time. Among those whose feasts we celebrate today are our own dear parents and loved ones, teachers and priests who guided us along the way to sanctity, our unknown, unheralded neighbors and friends who knew God intimately and were known by Him. Father Lawrence in *The Week With Christ* reminds us: "Christ has been asking us to become saints all during the past liturgical year as we sang His praises. Today, naturally, He emphasizes the invitation. Come to Me, He says, come all the way—hold back nothing. That means sacrifice—giving up our own wills to follow His, putting our sacrifice on the altar and saying to Christ: You do my wanting for me...Now, Christ's wanting for us might include sickness, suffering, death for ourselves or our loved ones...it is the work of a lifetime. Our giving of ourselves is all He needs to make saints of us. He does the rest."

INTROIT

So, "Let us all rejoice in the Lord," bid the words of today's Mass, "as we celebrate this feast in honor of all the saints, a day upon which the angels rejoice and praise the Son of God." The psalm verse (*Psalm* 32:1) continues this same thought: "Rejoice in the Lord, you (who are) just; praise befits the upright."

The music for this Introit is used also on the feast of our Lady of Mount Carmel, as also on the feasts of St. Anne, St. Agatha, St. Thomas of Canterbury, and others. Hear the joy in *Gaudeamus*, reaching up from earth to heaven where *Domino* reigns. *Diem festum celebrantes* is little more than a statement, but see how we are lifted up as we *honore Sanctorum omnium*. The angels, rejoicing in heaven (*gaudent angeli*) remind us that our joy should not be boisterous, but mildly temperate. *Collaudant* once more brings us to honor God in heaven, but note how reverent is the music on *Filium Dei*. The emphasis of the music on *Domino* and again on *Dei* shows us that, while it is a feast of all the saints, it is primarily a feast of our Lord, who has brought the saints to heaven with Him. The "just" and the "upright" rejoice on earth today with the prayer and the hope that they, too, may one day be united in the Church Triumphant.

GRADUAL — Psalm 33:10-11.

"Let all you who are His saints fear the Lord, for nothing is wanting to those who fear Him. Those who seek the Lord shall not be deprived of any good."

The music for *Timete* is not fearful, but simply a calm reminder. The *Dominum* assures us that God is not someone with a big stick waiting to strike us, but One who is fully aware of all that happens to us on earth; and that assurance lifts us up at *omnes sancti*, because we are His saints on earth. Then hear the assurance of this truth in *quoniam nihil deest*—to those who bow down in humility in doing His will (*timentibus eum*). The same thought is repeated in the music of *inquirentes autem Dominum*, where we have in the music a picture of those who search the heavens, as it were, to discover God's will; they shall not, even though they are still down on earth, be deprived of earthly blessings (*omni bono*).

ALLELUIA — Matthew 11:28.

After the *Alleluias* we find that beautiful invitation from our Lord, "Come to Me all you who labor and are burdened, and I will give you rest." In the invitation to "Come," see how gently the music leads us up from the earth to the heights of heaven. Again, the music reminds us that God is always mindful of what is happening to us, weighed down with *laboratis* and *onerati*; and although the music of *reficiam* is a repetition of the *Alleluia*, yet see how aptly it describes the heavenly rest that is promised. The saints followed the advice of our Lord, and were truly poor in spirit, meek, pure of heart, merciful, charitable and patient, with their eyes always on God in heaven. Today they are not only exemplars, but interceding for us, too, to learn that lesson as they did.

OFFERTORY — Wisdom 3:1-2,3.

"The souls of the just are in the hands of God, and the torment of death shall not touch them. In the sight of the unwise, they appeared to perish, but they are in peace, alleluia." This Offertory is taken from the Common of two or more martyrs, third setting. The music also is used for the Offertory on the feast of St. Michael, September 29. There is a fine parallel between the two feasts—both of saints now with God—showing how aptly the music fits the similar ideas. In *justorum animae* we see the souls of the just hovering between heaven and earth, since all of us are, by our union with God, ever *in manu Dei*. But those souls in heaven (*illos*) are not touched by the *tormentum malitiae* which does truly torment souls on earth. Note how earthy are the *oculis insipientium*.

The music on the word *autem* must surprise some when they study it for the first time; it has a very reasonable explanation: *autem* could be translated in this instance as, "however, they are wrong"; or "indeed, such is not the case here"; or again, "but with the souls reigning gloriously in heaven"; then we can see why it is so jubilant, why it reaches so far up in pure joy. Compare the peaceful music of *in pace* with those same two words at the end of the Communion on the feast of Christ the King. Again we have the promise of eternal peace, made joyful by the addition of an *alleluia*.

Have you ever stopped to think how often the liturgy keeps before our eyes the message of peace? Not only in the common of each day's Mass is there prayer after prayer for peace in the souls of God's children, but reminders, too, teaching us how we may put peace into our lives. On most of the feasts, too, this same idea is repeated over and over for our benefit. Surely it is no fault of holy Mother Church if we, her children, do not abide in peace throughout our lives! An unusually prosperous business man was asked recently how, in the midst of his great activities, he could always be so calm. He had a very simple answer, one which every Catholic should easily understand (and he was a Jewish gentleman): "Love God!" In that way lies peace.

COMMUNION - Matthew 5:8-10.

As the Communion, with its beautiful text from today's Gospel, is sung, our souls, filled with the grace of God's presence in holy Communion, can feel the value of our Lord's instruction: "The pure of heart are blessed; the peacemakers, too; and so,

likewise, are they who uncomplainingly withstand persecution."
As we saw in the Gradual today, God is aware of all that is happening to us; He sees our trials and difficulties. He does not gloat
over them, but rather permits them in order the better to perfect
us for our eternal life with Him. The *beati mundo corde* and *beati
pacifici* show the beatitude of heaven, while each *quoniam* gives
us a picture of the blessings coming down from heaven to earth
to the pure of heart and the peaceful. But now there seems to be
even a great happiness for those who suffer persecution in the
third *beati*, because such (*ipsorum*), even while on earth, belong
to the kingdom of heaven.

What a joyful tribute of praise to God should arise from our
hearts and voices today because of the glory He has given to
our fellow-members now in heaven, and because of what He is
doing each day for us. "Let us all rejoice in the Lord as we celebrate this feast! Let us bow down before Him, giving blessing
and glory and wisdom and thanksgiving and power and strength
to our God forever and ever. Amen."

In *Gregorian Chant*[1] Willi Apel says:

"Intimate relationship between melody and text is a trait so fundamental in Gregorian chant that it needs no substantiation. Relationship, however, is not the same as dependency or subjection. While it is true in certain types of chant, such as the recitation tones or the psalm tones, the melody is nothing more than a means to achieve a clear and impressive delivery of the text, it is equally undeniable that in many other cases the music assumes a degree of autonomy not dissimilar to that which exists in an aria by Bach or in a song by Schubert. In a Gradual, Alleluia, or Offertory, word and song join hands in the rendition of the liturgical prayer, one contributing the thought, the other what Thomas Aquinas called the *exsultatio mentis, de aeternis habita, prorumpens in vocem*—'the exultation of the mind, derived from things eternal, bursting forth in sound.' It is not without interest to notice that in the early centuries of Christian worship music occasionally exercised this function completely independent of a text. St. Augustine (as well as other Church Fathers) repeatedly expressed the idea that the highest rejoicing of the soul calls for music without words: 'If somebody is full of joyful exultation... he bursts out in an exulting song without words;' or: 'For whom is this jubilation more proper than for the nameless God...And since you cannot name Him and yet may not remain silent, what else can you do but break out in jubilation so that your heart may rejoice without words, and that the immensity of your joy may not know the bounds of syllables.' Such wordless jubilations of great extension, including up to three hundred notes, occur in Ambrosian chant. Although nominally attached to the syllable of a word, they actually attain independent status as purely musical formations. No vocalizations of comparable length exist in the Gregorian repertory, but there is only a difference of degree, not of essence, between the endless Ambrosian *melodiae* and the fairly extended melismas so frequently found in Gregorian chant, particularly in the Graduals and in the verses of the Offertories. They are the most obvious indication of the fact that the music

[1] Indiana University Press.

of the chant stands in the relationship of a peer, not of a servant, to the text.

"Several of the outstanding Gregorianists, as well as many of their 'minor brethren,' have attributed to certain chants specific expressive values derived from the text or related to the occasion. Thus, Gevaert finds that in the Antiphon *Ecce ancilla Domini: fiat mihi secundum verbum tuum* (Behold the handmaid of the Lord: be it done unto me according to Thy word; Luke 1:38) 'the melodic line, sweetly bowing until the end of the chant, renders with a charming naivety the profound reverence of the Virgin before the messenger of God.' To Frere, the Responsory *Angelus Domini apparuit Joseph*...(The angel of the Lord appeared unto Joseph...; Matthew 1:20) 'represents the quiet appearance of the angel to Abraham on Mt. Moriah.' Gerold sees in the first two melismas of the Tract *Commovisti, Domine, terram, et conturbasti eam* (Thou hast made the earth to tremble; Thou hast broken it; Ps. 60:2) 'the tendency to express in music the action of the Eternal shaking the earth.' Johner feels that in the Communion *Vox in Rama audita est, ploratus et ululatus: Rachel plorans filios suos noluit consolari, quia non sunt* (In Rama was there a voice heard, lamentation, and weeping, and great mourning, Rachel weeping for her children, and would not be comforted, because they are not; Matthew 2:18) 'the inception on the fifth of the mode, the emphasis on the dominant and the *pressus* over *ploratus* are expressions of gripping sorrow; they almost sound like a shrill outcry,' while at the end 'through this harmony (close on d'-b-g) the grief is tempered.' Ferretti feels that in the Antiphon *Montes Gelboe* 'the melodic line of *Quomodo*, with its descent from the dominant to the tonic, is an excellent rendition of David's stupor upon hearing the horrible news' (of Saul's and Jonathan's death; 2 Samuel 1:21-23)....

"Nobody will question the right, if not the duty, of Catholic writers to interpret the chants in such a way as to bring them close to the minds and hearts of the faithful. Descriptive explanations designed to achieve this goal have, no doubt, a legitimate place in books of a popularizing nature where, in fact, they are found in great number."

The following excerpts from articles on plain chant, by Rt. Rev. Michael Chapman, appeared in *The Acolyte* many years ago. They are still apt, and will undoubtedly serve as excellent material for those who are teaching chant, as well as for parish choirmasters and organists:

In his *History of Plain Chant*, Dr. Peter Wagner gives us a general survey of the types of chant that form the base of liturgical church music.

The oldest writer on music who speaks of the liturgical chant of his time, Aurelian of Rome, of the 9th century, puts together in the last (20th) chapter of his *Musica disciplina* the different forms of the Mass music, and discusses them in the order in which they come in the Mass. He says: "The Office of the Mass consists in the first place of Antiphons which are called Introits. They received the name from being sung at the entrance of the people into the basilica, and the singing lasted until the pontiff and the other ecclesiastical dignitaries in their rank have entered the church in regulated order, and have occupied the places belonging to them. Then the Litany is sung, in which God and Christ are entreated to have mercy upon the people; after which the priest, in imitation of the angel who announced Glory to God in the highest, and on earth peace to men of good will, begins this very song.

"Next is chanted the Responsory, which is called the Gradual, after the steps (*gradus*) from which it is sung: because among the ancients the singers, like the speakers, used to take their place on such raised steps. Hence we speak also of the Gradual Psalms, which, according to the literal interpretation, are so called because they were sung from the steps. The Alleluia we received from the Jews, to whose language the word belongs. It means 'Praise God,' and out of reverence it was not translated into any other language; it is very fittingly sung before the Gospel, that the minds of the faithful may be prepared by this song for the reception of the words of Salvation.

"The chant which the Church sings to the Lord over the oblations offered is called the Offertory. This custom is an imitation of the ancient Fathers to whom was given the direction: When a feast and festal day is celebrated, then ye shall sound trumpets over your sacrifices, and your memorial shall be before the Lord. At the administration of Communion, the *Agnus Dei qui tollis peccata mundi, miserere nobis* is first sung, that the faithful, who partake of the Body and Blood of the Lord, may with the uplifting of their voice praise that which they receive in their mouth, and in order that they may honor Him who is turned into bodily food for them to taste, and who, as the Church teaches, came down to be crucified, to die, and to be buried. At its conclusion, yet another chant is sung, which is called the Communion, so that while the people are receiving the heavenly blessing, their souls may be exalted and uplifted by sweet chanting to sublime contemplation."

These were the chants of the Mass in the ninth century in Gaul and in Rome, for in the time of Aurelian the liturgy prevailing in Gaul was the Roman. He does not mention the Tracts, because they were alternatives to the Alleluia; but they already existed in the ninth century. In the same way the *Sanctus* is passed over, probably because it belongs originally to the Preface with which it is immediately connected, as may still be recognized in the case of its oldest melody. The *Credo* on the other hand was not yet included in the liturgy of Rome in the ninth century as a Mass-chant, and it is on the whole the latest chant of the Mass. However, its musical arrangement, as Aurelian depicts it, is older than the ninth century; it rests upon the liturgical measures taken by Gregory the Great (604), and is inseparably bound up with his settlement of the liturgy of the Mass.

If we glance at the chants individually, they are seen to fall into two well-defined groups. The oldest go back to the *psalmody* and were originally whole psalms; they differ from one another only in their musical execution. To the responsorial Mass-chants belong the Gradual responsory and the Alleluia; to the Antiphonal, the Introit, Offertory and Communion. The Tract forms an exception, as it was sung later by the singer, without repetitions by the choir, straight through from beginning to end. These three forms have to this day never disguised the fact that they owe their origin to the psalms or the canticles. The other groups of

Mass-chants are more like hymns, and some of them are actually called hymns, as for example *Hymnus Angelicus* (*Gloria in excelsis*), etc. The psalmodic parts of the Mass music have varying texts: as a rule each Mass has its own text for the Introit, Gradual, Alleluia (or Tract), Offertory and Communion. They are therefore called the Proper. The other group never changes its texts; for this reason it was placed in contrast to the Proper as the Ordinary of the Mass; it includes the *Kyrie*, *Gloria*, *Credo*, *Sanctus* and *Agnus Dei.*

The contrast in character between the Proper and the Ordinary is shown in their liturgical position, as well as in the manner of their execution. The chants of the Proper are early enough to form part of the arrangement of the Mass made by Gregory the Great; they form an essential constituent part of the Mass, so that there is no such thing as a Mass without Introit, without Gradual, without Alleluia (or Tract) etc. (except the last days of Holy Week and the Easter Vigil, which liturgically stand on a peculiar footing). The significance of any particular feast is much more clearly shown in the varying elements which compose the Proper; for example, it is often the case that the Introit at once leads the way, with a dramatic vividness, into the realm of thought belonging to the feast. Further, the pieces of the Ordinary were of less value from the musical point of view. The Proper alone is contained in the oldest liturgical books of chant; it has formed the iron framework of the Mass music from Gregory's time to the present day.

The Ordinary, on the contrary, has a very changeful history to record. In Rome at first, it was sung not by the schola but by the ministers in assisting at the altar, or else by all the people, as was the favorite custom in Gaul. As the household of the Greek Popes of the seventh and eighth centuries contained also Greek clergy, this explains the fact, already mentioned, that these chants of the Ordinary were in many places also sung in Greek. The Roman origin of this custom is expressly shown by an ancient anonymous writer of Tours. On the other hand, the performance of these chants by the clergy had a reflex effect on their melodic form: this was at first quite simple and syllabic, and demanded no particular skill. From the moment when the choir of singers supplanted the clergy and people in their share of the chants of the Mass, and took over the execution of all liturgical chants, that is from the eleventh to the twelfth centuries, there began to appear in the chant books some melodies for the *Kyrie, Gloria*, etc., but they were set as a rule quite at the end, as evidence of their late adoption. These were rich and beautiful; accordingly the older and simpler ones were degraded to ordinary days and to Masses for the Dead.

An alteration of much importance, both liturgically and musically, was made when the papal singers of Avignon went to Rome with Gregory XI in 1377, and took with them the new art of harmonized chant which then flourished in France; from that time it gradually became the custom to sing the chants of the Ordinary in harmony. Strangely enough, the Ordinary thus composed in harmony was called simply, *"Missa"*: this reveals the fact that the Ordinary had become the principal part of the Mass from the musical point of view. This development did not bring with it any particular gain, for it is merely an unnatural circumstance that since then the chief emphasis artistically has rested on the chants of the Mass which do not necessarily belong to it and are, to some extent, liturgically superfluous. What a far more grateful field would have been offered to composers in the variable texts of the Proper, though, it is true, they would have been able to perform their works only once or twice during the year.

THE INTROIT

The earliest evidences of the Introit are found in the form of the *Psalmus Responsorius*. This form was already in vogue at Matins. In its original form it was an entire psalm sung with responsorial antiphon while the celebrant was entering the church in procession. Traces of this processional are found in earliest times. The antiphon took on more detailed "motif" form as feasts and seasons became more clearly defined. The first Antiphonary of Gregory contains Introits. The first Roman ordo of the sixth to seventh century contains instruction for their use. All rites, except the most Eastern, contain Introits. Litanies in procession are the basis of the Introit in the Eastern liturgies. The *Liber Pontificalis* ascribes the first definite Introit to Pope Celestine in the early fifth century. This same source ascribes the modulation of this "processional psalm responsory" to St. Gregory. Probst gives Pope Gelasius (492) the credit for this modulation. The actual time of its origin cannot be stated. We surmise from many references that this processional psalm was begun in the first century, because during the sojourn in the catacombs we find references to curtailment because of the short procession to the crypts.

After the persecutions, there was free development until the modulation or curtailment of the last of the fifth, middle of the sixth century. The first Roman ordo states that this processional psalm should cease with the end of the procession. We find it definitely in its present form in the eleventh century as by this time the processions were also curtailed. This history is as definite as can be ascertained at present. The one certain point is its form, i.e., a psalm with responsorial antiphon. This is really the form today with but one verse of the psalm with the lesser doxology.

The texts of the Introit are, as usual in the Proper, from the Psalter, and Scriptures; the Great Codex of St. Gall and the "Paleography" of Solesmes gives us chants for 203 Masses. These melodies are choral in scope and conception; the psalm verse is also more ornate than the congregational and canonical chants. The antiphon and verse construction follow a definite plan, e.g., if the antiphon is the first verse of a psalm, the verse of the Introit is the next verse. If the antiphon selects a middle verse, the verse will then be the first verse of the psalm. This is logical since the Introit, as previously stated, contained the whole or greater part of a psalm with responsorial antiphon.

THE GRADUAL RESPONSORY

Our Mass today contains two chants between the Lessons of Scripture (Epistle and Gospel). Originally there were three Lessons, the Prophetic, Epistle and Gospel, with a responsory following the first and second. The first (prophetic) Lesson was eliminated in the fifth century, but both chants were retained. Relics of the three Lessons at Mass are found today in certain days of Lent and in the Ember-day Masses. Wagner in his *Intro-*

ductions cites the importance of these Gradual chants in that both were retained, even though one Lesson was dropped.

The Gradual Responsory is the oldest and most important of the musical parts of the Mass. It dates in its first form, that of "responsorial solo," from apostolic times. The custom was a direct heritage from the Jews, i.e., of singing an entire psalm with congregational refrain between Lessons. Another noteworthy fact is that the Gradual is the only musical part of the Mass that is there for its own sake, as all action ceases, and not as an accompaniment to other actions, as is the case with the Introit, Offertory, and other chants. From apostolic times until the middle of the fifth century the Gradual Responsory was an entire psalm with congregational refrain. To cite Dr. Wagner again:

"That the Responsorium of the Mass at the first comprised a whole psalm is shown beyond doubt by several statements, particularly some of St. Augustine. The precentor sang in turn the verses of the psalm for the day, and the congregation answered each verse with the refrain. In his sermon 176, St. Augustine explains: 'We have heard the first Lesson; then we sang the psalm in which we mutually incited one another by singing with one voice and one heart: O come let us worship!' The last words formed the refrain sung by the congregation to the part of the soloist. He is still more explicit at the beginning of his exposition of Psalm 119: 'It is a short psalm which we have just heard sung and to which we have responded.' Longer psalms were also sung in their entirety, as may be concluded from his exposition of Psalm 138, which he begins thus: 'I had arranged that a shorter psalm should be sung by the lector; but he, as it appears, in a moment of perplexity performed another, and I preferred to follow the will of God shown in the error of the lector rather than my own. Accordingly if I have detained you somewhat by the length of the psalm (Psalm 138 has 24 verses), you must not blame me for it, but perceive that God does not put a strain upon us without benefit.'

"From this and other passages it seems to follow that the refrain of the congregation always comprised a whole verse. In his exposition of Psalm 43, Augustine mentions as the refrain, *Inimici mei dixerunt mala mihi, quando morietur et peribit nomen ejus* (v.6): in the *Ennarratio* 2 of Psalm 29: *Exaltabo te Domine quoniam suscepisti me, nec iucundasti inimicos meos super me* (the opening verse); in the exposition of Psalm 25: *Ne perdas cum impiis animam, et cum viris sanguinum vitam meam.* This refrain is taken from the last part of the psalm (v.9), and confirms the above statement that the psalm was sung in its entirety.

"The evidence also shows that in the Roman Mass, before its regulation by Gregory the Great, the soloist performed a whole psalm. In the third sermon on the anniversary of his accession, Leo the Great (440-461) says: 'We have sung the Davidical psalm (the 109th), not for our own exaltation but to the glory of Christ the Lord.' "

As in all forms of Mass music, the introduction of more florid chants came with the delegation of this work to choirs. As this began in the fourth century, we find the use of an entire psalm gave way to an ornate solo chant, with a responsory. For some time, several verses of a psalm were used, but the florid melodies made this part of the service unduly long so that further curtailment followed. A relic of a "several-verse Gradual" is found in the arrangement of the *Haec Dies* with verses that is now used for the entire octave of Easter. Formerly, this entire work was the Gradual for Easter Sunday alone.

The change to the present type of Gradual, i.e., solo chant with responsory and verse, began at the close of the sixth century with St. Gregory and was completed by the eleventh century. In the thirteenth century we find the custom of eliminating the solo and responsorial idea, and it was confirmed as a straight choir-chant. The Council of Trent confirms this in the sixteenth century. In the early days of solo chant, the celebrant appointed the soloist, who was always a deacon. St. Gregory delegated this to subdeacons and those in minor orders. Traces of two and four chanters are found already in the seventh century, thus early presaging the use of these melodies as a choir chant, with verse only.

There are 118 Graduals in the Codices, all of them from the psalms, except thirteen that are taken from the New Testament, and one from an outside source, that of the dedication of a church. The oldest Masses "*de Tempore*" are, of course, from the

psalms. The ornate and rich melodies with their splendid form
give proof of the care and regard of the early Church for this
part of the service. As is well known, the name comes from the
steps leading up to the recitation of the lessons and was sung
by the soloists on the lower step of the ambo. We can readily
understand its importance as one of the most effective parts of
the Mass that were devoted to the catechumens, and as a natural
sequence, that some of its importance is lost today because this
distinction, i.e., catechumens, is no longer maintained.

THE ALLELUIA WITH VERSE

The Alleluia, today, is the second chant between Lessons. In
its early form it is the responsory to the psalm verses. At a very
early time the Alleluia was clothed with a rich melismatic melody, and was used earlier than the fourth century at Bethlehem
and in Grecian liturgies.

St. Jerome, urging its introduction into the Roman Mass,
gives us evidence of this. Pope Damasus (368-384) introduced it
into the Roman Mass at the instance of St. Jerome. At first its
use was confined to Easter but spread quickly to the entire Easter
season. In regulating its place in the Roman liturgy, Gregory
(Epistle IX:12) ordered it for the entire year, except on penitential days and fast days. Just when the entire psalm was shortened to one or two verses is not known, but this was already
established at the time of the Gregorian settlement. It is truly a
"*cantus responsorius*." The cantor intones the *Alleluia*; the choir
repeats it; the cantor chants the verse, with the responsory *Alleluia* again sung by choir.

THE COMMUNION

One of the very old chants of the Mass is the Communion
Antiphon with verse, a responsorial chant sung during the reception of holy Communion by the faithful. We have the authori-
ty of all the liturgies, Eastern and Western, including the testimony of the Apostolic Constitutions, that Psalm 33 was the
antiphon and verses for the Communion. St. Augustine introduced it at the same time that the Offertory antiphon was added
to the Mass in the African Church. It was, up to the seventh

century, the entire Psalm 33 with *Gloria Patri*. It was sung by schola and clergy. The earliest Roman chant books exhibit a change from Psalm 33; other texts, introduced until the eighth Sunday after Pentecost, alone contain the verses of the old Psalm 33, i.e., "*Gustate et videte.*" From the eleventh century the verses were curtailed as general Communion seems not to have been the universal practice on the great feasts; and in the twelfth century we have manuscripts of Masses without the Communion verse—merely the antiphon.

Historians agree that of all forms of the Mass the Communion was preserved more certainly against interpolations and [was held intact longer] in mid-continental Europe than in any part of the world. It may be noted here that the Carthusian monks have preserved all forms free from abuses. We have evidence of this in our own section, as the monks of Gethsemani Abbey were never afflicted with the Medicean or Mechlin chant versions. From the fourteenth century all Communion verses were omitted and but one remains today, that of the Requiem Mass. Of the 147 different Communion antiphons, 80 are from Sacred Scripture, 64 from the psalms, and 4 have allusions only to texts of the Scriptures. In nature, form, and rendition the Communion is almost identical with the Introit, even to the idea of imparting a "motif." In this instance the "motif" is not introductory but more as a matter of "recollection" of the principal idea of the feast or season just celebrated. Furthermore, the interpretative analysis of these "motifs" exhibits a sort of reflected loveliness in contrast to the brilliancy of orientation of the Introit and Graduals.